/ 50

MW01254917

ANOTHER VAGABOND LOST TO LOVE
BERLIN STORIES

———

Travel Essays and Poetry
on leaving & arriving

by Charlotte Eriksson
The Glass Child

ANOTHER VAGABOND LOST TO LOVE
BERLIN STORIES
Travel essays and poetry
on leaving & arriving
***

Copyright © 2015 | All Rights Reserved
Charlotte Eriksson
Broken Glass Records: Press & Distribution
www.CharlotteEriksson.com

DISCOGRAPHY
Charlotte Eriksson EP, *2011*
I Will Lead You Home *single, 2011*
This Is How Ghosts Are Made EP, *2011*
Songs of An Insomniac EP, *2011*
I'd Like To Remain A Mystery, *LP 2013*
Empty Roads & Broken Bottles: in search for The Great Perhaps, book *2013*
I'd Like To Remain A Mystery *Acoustic Edition, 2013*
Love Always, Your Tragedy EP, *2013*
I Must Be Gone, or Stay and Die, LP *2014*
Another Vagabond Lost To Love, book 2015
Dear Me, One Day I'll Make You Proud, book 2015

ANOTHER VAGABOND LOST TO LOVE

Another Vagabond Lost To Love

6 months, 2 weeks, 4 days,
and I still don't know which month it was then
or what day it is now.
Blurred out lines
from hangovers
to coffee,
another vagabond
lost to love.

I felt the storm through my walls last night
and the lighting turned the lights off.
But I don't know why they all closed their doors
'cause I collected my hopes and wandered by the edge of the water
to see the way nature never gets off track,
and I've never seen the world so awake
and full of life
'cause it's mostly static. It's mostly still.
But there was chaos like a hurricane
blowing things up in the air
and it looked a lot like it does in me
these days,
behind my ribcage,
and it gave me peace. The way there was order within the storm
for weather has a reason, and
all
must
pass.

4am alone and on my way.

These are my finest moments.

And it's such a shame no one can see me now,

'cause if they did I swear they would all lift their sights from that safe grey ground and nod their heads and say "she's on her way" and no one would doubt me like they always do around here,

around me.

But then again, if anyone did see me I bet I wouldn't walk like I do now,

or sing like I do

now,

like thoughts free flow straight out with the winds

and no one holds me back here,

or tells me where to turn.

This road all mine to keep

and it will last for as long I want it to,

like a sinner stolen by the Gods

and I am not sorry.

I scrub my skin

to rid me from

you

and I still don't know why I cried.

It was just something in the way you took my heart and rearranged my insides and I couldn't recognise the emptiness you left me with when you were done. Maybe you thought my insides would fit better this way, look better this way, to you and us and all the rest.

But then you must have changed your mind

or made a wrong

because why did you

leave?

6 months, 2 weeks, 4 days,
and I still don't know which month it was then
or what day it is now.
I replace cafés with crowded bars and empty roads with broken
bottles
and this town is healing me slowly but still not slow or fast enough
because there is no right way to do this.

There is not right way to do this.

There is no right way to do this.

"FEAR URGED HIM TO GO BACK, BUT GROWTH DROVE HIM ON."

— JACK LONDON, WHITE FANG

Dear You,

You who have ever read my words online, shared a quote with a
friend, sent me beautiful little messages now and then, or just a
thought a lonely night in June …
To you who have listened to my music, bought my CDs,
my last book or just this one …
YOU are the reason to why this book exists.
YOU are the reason to why I exist.

I am nothing alone.
Thank you for letting me do what my heart tells me to.
♥

XXX

It's the beating of my heart.

The way I lie awake, playing with shadows slowly climbing up my wall. The gentle moonlight slipping through my window and the sound of a lonely car somewhere far away, where I long to be too, I think. It's the way I thought my restless wandering was over, that I'd found whatever I thought I had found, or wanted, or needed, and I started to collect my belongings. Build a home. Safe behind the comfort of these four walls and a closed door.

Because as much as I tried or pretended or imagined myself as a part of all the people out there,

I was still the one locking the door every night.

Turning off the phone and blowing out the candles so no one knew I was home.

'cause I was never really well around the expectations of my personality

and I wanted to keep to myself.

and because I haven't been very impressed lately.

By people,

or places.

Or the way someone said he loved me and then slowly changed his mind.

I'm easily bored and it's comfortable to let the safety of a place drag you in. In with its routines and circles, habits of being content. Of not wanting more. I might have fallen for its shelter a little while, because the winter was hard and cold and I was small and alone, but my heart never did. It had been screaming in silence every night, trying to get my attention. But I was too busy being sad, or bored. Just unimpressed by it all. And some days I couldn't tell the difference between the beating of a heart and the dying of one.

It all takes time and lessons and places, but I'm learning to listen to my restless heart, telling me to "go, go, go!"
  because I was never meant to stay
    or settle.
I am running and singing and when it's raining I'm the only one left on the open street, smiling with my eyes fixed on the sky because it's cleansing me. I'm the one on the other side of the party, hearing laughter and the emptying of bottles while I peacefully make my way to the river, a lonely road, following the smell of the ocean. I'm the one waking up at 4am to witness the sunrise, where the sky touches the sea, and I hold my elbows, grasping tight to whatever I've made of myself. And then nights like these, sitting high on adrenaline in the dark by a tiny lake somewhere I don't know where it is, for I was running and deliberately lost my way. The world far off and nothing but my breath and the very next step and it's like hypnosis. The feeling of conquering my own aliveness with no task but to keep going, making every way the right away,

        and that's a metaphor for everything.

There's this thing they say, about living according to your nature, your natural ability to get by. When you place yourself in an environment with tasks and challenges that the universe didn't intend for you to do or take on, everything aspires to take you away from there. You need an incredible amount of self-control to become good at something you're not meant to do. It's possible, but your subconscious will constantly be asking you to leave. It will consume you with a constant feeling of doubt, of negotiating with yourself because you want to do this, you tell yourself, but still you need to remind yourself of WHY every second of every day, because it doesn't come naturally, doesn't come easy, and you will always be working against the world, against your nature. No flow. No wind in the back. Uphill climb with stones on the road.

There are days when the loneliness eats me like cancer and I can't find one single reason to keep running, keep searching, hustling, creating. But deep inside this mind of mine, I know. I always know. And there is no turning back. There is no alternative. This is the place I've been given and been made for, and someone's got to fill it. So you need to ask yourself: will you keep resisting the place you've been given, ignore the signs and find excuses for everything, just to get by? Or will you surrender to fate, trust your story and take your place so proud and sure that no one will ever doubt that that place was made for you and you only, like it in fact was?

Answers are simple when you ask the right questions and I was not born to slow down. It's me alone in front of whatever God or spirit there is and the nights I run far off track, in doubt or in fear, I must believe that it's in the dark we learn how to feel. Because sometimes it's not about seeing where the path will lead, but to feel it, and that's where I will go. I can choose to ignore or avert, but there will be hurdles on my way, redirecting me back to my place, and I need to take responsibility for it.

So I keep going. Keep doing. Keep being. **This**. I let it consume me, the same old feeling of wheeling alone on this road

    that turned into my life. My story.

        The endless pursuit of peacefulness and belonging.

        A quest towards happiness with nothing but life itself,
and I am right back off track, where all things of meaning happen.

        As long as I am moving, I'm right on the path I made.

The Wanderess

You risked your life, didn't you.
Sharpened your skills, mastered the sword from every angle
and made your plans.
Marched straight on without looking back
and so now tell me—what did it lead to?

Where are you now?

You left the ones who said no and ran uphill at midnight to howl
with the wolves and the moon
and the night was profound, the sky all yours to keep.
You made your pact with the Gods and the lords
and promised to soldier on.
Designed your life accordingly.
No objects to distort or people to distract,
and did you get what you wanted?
Did it lead you to your goal?
Are you still on your way?
Still glorious beyond belief?
Blood still flowing? *Barely.*
World still growing?
Real or in your head?

Listen:
imagine a stage.
A crowd full of painted faces, excited to escape
for an hour or two.
Bodies.
Imagine a dancer. Behind the curtains. Nervous but ready.

Practised for years, days and nights, in and out
to get every muscle tight, every movement right, every corner of
every star involved and she's ready.
She will take the stage and she will take their breath away.
They will go home at night announcing "oh, what a stunning show,"
and go to bed
with someone they love
and go to work the next day
and maybe give a thought to the dancer in a day or two
and so that's that.

(*what did it all lead up to?*)

Now take the dancer.
A night sky. An open field. Somewhere far away from the city.
Erase the crowd. Erase the audience, the judges, the need to express
or deliver or convince. Erase aching muscles because the dancer is
dancing when her heart tells her to, eating when hungry and sleeping
when tired, and it's all balanced and harmonised and there are no
distortions. No habits or ugly patterns.
"But that's impossible," you say, "not reality and no, that's
impossible."
I will not tell you what is impossible, but what is
in fact
possible
and what I do know is that the dancer will never dance as gracefully
as when there is no one around to see and she will not care. What I
do know is that the night when the crowd goes home, pleased and
enjoyed, the dancer might just not and what I do know is that

    I gave my life.
Rebuilt and redesigned
and the crowd is pleased
from time to time,

going home humming "what a lovely show"
    but I am not
           pleased,
and what I do know is that I will never sing as gracefully as when no one is around
and that is what makes it graceful,
and I will not tell you what is impossible but what
in fact
is possible
and it is possible to get everything you ever thought you wanted and realise
it is not enough.
What if everything is not enough.
    (What did it all lead up to?)

Now place me on an open field.
A night sky,
far away from the city.
Erase the crowd. Erase the audience, the judges, the need to express or deliver or convince. Erase aching hearts because I love when there is something to love, sing when I have a song to sing, and write when I have something to write.
It's all balanced and harmonised and there are no distortions. No habits or ugly patterns
and I will tell you that this
is what is
in fact
enough.

So, this is for us.
This is for us who sing, write, dance, act, study, run and love
and this is for doing it even if no one will ever know
because the beauty is in the act of doing it,

16

not in what it can lead to.

This is for the times I lose myself while writing, singing, playing

and no one is around and they will never know

but I will forever remember

and that shines brighter than any praise or fame or glory I will ever have,

and this is for you who write or play or read or sing

by yourself with the light off and door closed

when the world is asleep and the stars are aligned

and maybe no one will ever hear it

or read your words

or know your thoughts

but it doesn't make it less noble.

It makes it ethereal. Mysterious.

Infinite.

For it belongs to you and whatever God or spirit you believe in

and only you can decide how much it meant

and means

and will forever mean

to you,

and other people will experience it too

through you.

Through your spirit. Through the way you talk.

Through the way you walk and love and laugh and care

and I never meant to write this long

but what I want to say is:

Don't try to present your art by making other people read or hear or see or touch it: make them feel it. Wear your art like your heart on your sleeve and keep it alive by making people feel a little better. Feel a little lighter. Create art in order for yourself to become yourself and let your very existence be your song, your poem, your story. Let your very identity be your book.

Let the way people say your name sound like the sweetest melody.

So go create. Take photographs in the woods, run alone in the rain
and sing your heart out high up on a mountain
where no one will ever hear
and your very existence will be the most hypnotising scar.
Make your life be your art
            and you will never be forgotten.

On Leaving

I seek the city
because there is nothing sweeter than not being alone in your loneliness.

The Waking Up

They say the biggest enemy for a free mind is commitment, and I've been running
from it my whole life,
only to find myself in a life long commitment
to my running
away.

It starts like this: slow. You stop noticing. The habits grow and you build routines you don't acknowledge. You make your way through your daily tasks, passing the same people, crossing the same road, and when you look back by the end of the day you can barely remember how you got from here to there because it's all a blur. Because you weren't there. Your body works on autopilot while your mind can be somewhere else and that's how you set yourself up for a day in 30 years when you realise that your whole life passed you by, and you didn't even notice. You weren't even there.

I was free with every road as my home. No limitations and no commitments. But then summer passed and winter came and I fell short for safety. I fell for its spell, slowly humming me to sleep, because I was tired and small, too weak to take or handle those opinions and views, attacking me from every angle. Against my art, against my self, against my very way of living. I collected my thoughts, my few possessions and built isolated walls around my values and character. I protected my own definition of beauty and success like a treasure at the bottom of the sea, for no one saw what I saw, or felt the same as I did, and so I wanted to keep to myself.

You hide to protect yourself.

I was just a kid when I fled, from my home and my friends, and I was easily convinced. I swallowed words and rejections like pills I thought I had to take and I never questioned ugly thoughts about myself or my ways. I took them on and kept them safe behind my ribcage, repeating ugliness every night I tried to sleep and everywhere I went,

and someone should have told me right there and then to throw them off, here and now, before it's too late. Like flames on my skin for they will burn and kill one day, so run run run far away!

But no one did, so I kept swallowing them whole, taking stranger's opinions to cover up my own and that is the beginning of the rapture.

The slow fade of a once-strong mind.

But see, I am not a kid, anymore, for I've seen things, felt things, done things, and I wandered everywhere and nowhere, seeking balance or unbalance, for I was not. I was unsettled. Unrested but restless and I found my own ways to fight. My own ways to define. And my ways may not suit you or them or anyone else but see, that is my point: who wrote the rule-book for how a life ought to be lived? And why doesn't anyone question it?

This is my fight for freedom of thought. To define love and beauty, safety and art according to my own standards. What makes sense to me, within my own ways on this path I'm creating as I go along. How I'm living and who I want to be.

So I found my own ways to define and I found my own reason. Kept it hidden well like a realisation the others wouldn't understand. Locked away, for people are attacking me like wolves around here, every angle during every storm. Throwing words against my art and my bones and my value of a home, and so I hid away. Kept it safe behind four walls.

(You hide to protect yourself)

But see, hiding is just a decorated way of giving up, surrendering, not taking the climb. Because it's simple. Lazy.

I hid away. Fell short for safety behind four walls, and it was nice, I guess, for a while, with all these keys and locks and possessions. People around but still not very close, for I tried to act accordingly but never really fit. I observed their routines, saying hi and then goodnight. How to walk and sleep and eat, and I tried to act accordingly. Drowned my restless mind and wanderlust in darker liquids, burning sweet in my throat. That worked for a while, but still not long enough, so I took to medication or any other kind of empty label you'd like to throw at it. I went to churches and temples, practiced meditation like a priest in pain with no salvation in hand. I sat quiet, cross-legged on the ground for six days straight to drown out the voices in order to hear my own. But the noises were still out there at the end of the day, and so I smoked and drank and sang and ran. Joined running teams and kept running with blood in my throat and screams in my brain, for I was in pain.

Back to my house. Back to my four walls:
I stayed longer in bed every morning, staring at the ceiling but still somewhere further away. I learned the sound of every person in that house where I lived, waiting patiently until they had emptied the ways and I could sneak out the door before I had to meet anyone or anything for I didn't have a lot to say, anymore, or sing, or write, and I was dried up. A songwriter with no songs to write. A singer with no voice to use. I'm a writer and I do write, but in the morning when I'm sober again the words are left as a messy storm on the paper and I can barely remember what I tried to say.

It starts like this. Your protect yourself in habits that turn into movements your body does, and it's astonishing to observe the way your muscles move and work with your mind in rest, for you have memorised the patterns. You don't even have to think, anymore, about anything. Wake, walk, straight line, take bus, say hi, do tasks, go home, lie down. No mind or heart or ecstasy needed to make it through these days, and sometimes that's all you want. It's easy to stay like this. It's comfortable. Simple. No effort. You can pass decades like this because you simply just go on, and after some years of stormy weather and battling on your own, the 'just going on' part seems pretty damn good.

But then it's my heart. The way it never had enough. The way it's longing and yearning and screaming because this is not my nature. This is not what I came here for and I am a hunted animal, never settled in myself

and I believe in fate and star crossed lovers and I am not done.

I believe you only get a few moments in your life, when things finally stop. The noises, the running, the constant nagging somewhere deep in your throat. When you've been glancing at that door for weeks, months, and one day you're just ready. You know what you have to do. So you stand up, straight back, as if you're preparing for a battle with all the enemies you've ever had, and walk with light but determined steps toward that god damn door. You look at it for a while, as some sort of goodbye, and then you close it. No drama, no loud noises. Just calmly close the door, turn around, back to your desk, take up that new journal, and then you start. Goodbyes are beginnings of everything.

A goodbye is the beginning of everything.

There comes a time when you're ready to embrace the new beginning the universe has laid out for you, and when you are, nothing can stand in your way. And YOU need to be brave enough to let your own strength guide you, and never look back.

I was done with my childish safety in comfort. I was done with my hiding away in order to protect myself, and ready to stand up for my own right to live my life. And that's when it all starts.

23

I Must Be Gone and Live,
Or Stay and Die
– Shakespeare, *Romeo & Juliet*

It had been a hard winter. The cold made me numb and small, unwilling to stand up and keep using my voice. Life played its play, leaving me in a town that was encircled by his name.

Memories in every corner.

But like the seasons come and go, the flowers slowly found their way through the soil, and as the air got crisper, the mornings lighter, I knew it was time. To let go. To keep moving. To start anew.

It was time to leave.

~~~

on Berlin

FEAR

So what is fear then?
Is it the quiet voice in your head,
observing but not saying a word.
The way eyes can speak more than words ever can,
and you see them watching. Observing.

Or is it the physical resistance it takes to make your way to that
room,
through that door, or simply out of bed
in the morning
Because you're scared.
  Of what?
Scared of living.
 Too wild
    and fall, fall, fall.
Free fall to the ground.
Or scared of not living at all, so you feel the pressure of every new
day.
Of how you have to capture,
make use of,
don't waste a single second because they could all be gone
tomorrow.

So how to free yourself from fear
without putting chains on your very own hands?
The way freedom never comes without commitments.
Because it's hard.
Trust me.
Being free is pretty damn hard.
A skill you need to learn.

How to wake up in the morning with all the endless possibilities and
not panic
because suddenly there are so many things you can do
and be
and feel
and not do
and not be
and not feel
so where to even start?

It's the way you lie in bed for three weeks straight,
waiting for the day when you will have regained all the strength you
lost but need
to simply leave.
Because leaving, too, is a skill.
Something you need to learn.
Practice.
Achieve.

And then one day,
how you open your eyes and you just leave.

And then you ask yourself, why the hell did it take you this long?

Somewhere in Europe, 2013

There is a difference between going somewhere and leaving something.
I was still just leaving.

***

We have not received your payment, Miss.
I shift my weight,
back and forth,
trying to find a salvation in between.
… we have not received your payment, Miss.
Please make the payment before this afternoon.
Yes, Sir, I will,
I say, and apologise silently in advance for not making the payment
this afternoon.
I go outside and the day is unfittingly beautiful.
It's spring and I'm broke.

I packed my bag again that evening,
fit my life inside a suitcase and left the key in the post-box.
The first train took me six hours, which was far from long enough,
for I was tired and needed somewhere to sleep and the train is zen-
like. Works in the same way the ocean does, the only place I dare to
close my eyes and trust the process, for I will get there without
trying. Wherever 'there' is.

      Trust the process,
         whatever that is.

***

It's 4.32am and I'm sitting by the desk in a cheap room in yet another hostel. I have this thing I do when I panic, a habit I can't quit, like smoking. I don't smoke, more than usual, but when I wake up I instantly find it hard to breathe, and that's what he did to me. Something is not right and my throat is too tight and I can't open the closet because it's too full of hidden pasts and I have this thing I do when I panic:

I run.

It takes four minutes to collect my belongings and throw my rucksack over my shoulder; 15 minutes to run with my lungs out of breath to the train station and two minutes to choose which train to take. It doesn't matter where it goes and the point is not to end up somewhere but to go there and I find tranquillity while going. On buses, trains, airplanes, cars – I'm going somewhere without having to fight with every fibre of my being to get there and I like the stillness, because it's rare, and I like the road.

So I did it again and now it's 4.37am and I'm sitting by the desk in a cheap room at a hostel. The clock is making thunders on the wall but it's a one-way threat because I have nowhere to go and no one to see and they never thought a lot of me but at least I did
but now I'm not so sure.

Now I'm not so sure.

JOURNAL I
IV.MMXIII

I wonder what will be left.
What they will say and know and think,
because it's a weird thought,
that this journey of mine is mine and mine only
and my feet walk on strange land every single day,
and most of the time I don't know what day or time or month it is
and it doesn't really matter.
   I'm breaking out of habits
'cause don Juan taught me how to live,
and I'd like to run with the great men, the free men,
so no human habits can stay.
   Like time.
      Like clinging.
   Or emotions you think you ought to feel.
So I rest my head when I can no longer stand
and wake up when I'm ready to begin again.
I don't eat until I'm hungry
and I try to listen to my restless little heart,
   as well as I know how to.

   I wonder what will be left.
What they will say and know and think and feel,
and if I'll remain a mystery.
   A myth they don't believe in.
Because this is my journey and mine only,
   and no one needs to listen
      if I learn to listen myself,
and I realise the only way to tell the others
   is through the way my voice can take these broken words

and turn them into music.
   Turn them into poetry.
And I sing to make myself come alive,
 but also for you,
because I'd like this to mean something.
To not disappear with the dark I will enter one day
 and so now I will tell.
If not for you, then for my own heart,
  because it tells me to,
    and I am learning to listen.

Summer 2013

I read Kerouac and slept on the beach, finding faults in everything that could be bought with money and praised everything that was free. I did not care what people thought or said or what would become of me, for I only had one single wish: to free myself from labels and names, that maybe I invented myself, in some ways, but never meant to. I studied the great masters, writers and philosophers. Practiced the teachings of Buddha, telling me to detach, not to cling. Learn oneness. But how to learn oneness when you're already as detached from yourself as one could be and still there I was, running into myself like a merry go round. I was tired of people calling out names as if it would be clues of who they spoke to, who they saw, who I was – but I was not. So I threw my baggage away, as to free myself from all they thought I was, and wandered childishly barefoot with a notebook and a guitar. I tried to shed my skin, take it back and in control, for other people owned it for so long and I was not theirs, anymore, and so I ran. For hours every morning before the city woke up, until my muscles screamed and refused to move and I refused to slow down for I was in pain. Kept running with tears in my eyes but a smile on my lips, telling me that **no one owns my body but me!** and soon they would see, too.

In my old naive ways I had thrown my phone in the river and wrote hand written letters to the ones I cared to write to, the ones I thought would understand one day, maybe, or at least try to.

I was back to my wandering.

I had wonderful nights, with skies so clear that the stars lit up the whole beach and it felt like they were all shining for me, lighting up my night. It might have been somewhere at the bottom of that wine the French old man at the market sold me every evening, and it might have been the way the bonfire sparked my brain or how I'd lost my ways, but either way it was simple, and I wanted simplicity.

A year ago I'd been 'the one'. The one who knew where she was going, what she wanted, how to get there and how to not. I'd been in love and was loved, but slowly, finally, it all grew into anger and regret, making me run from everything that wasn't freeing, burning, leading me to new land, new cities, wander foreign streets, because I couldn't stand the thought of all things past. I stood up and emptied the last bottle. I had decided not to regret anything and it taught me a lot, to love, to feel, to not live on my own for the first time. It taught me a lot about clinging and sadness and how to lose something you never thought you could live without, and how that was exactly what I did, now, anyway, despite of it all.

So a year ago I was 'the one', and now I slept under the bare sky because I was tired of being scared. Scared of what? Of this greedy world that can eat you alive. So according to my own ritual I turned myself in. Sold everything I couldn't fit in my suitcase and went out to become one with this universe because that's what I thought I had to do and so there I went.

I think there's something to be said about surrender. Stepping over to the other side. Because sometimes you're fighting against something that actually is on your side, if you just dare to give up your god damn pride and safety and human habits of unnecessary certainty. This world can be quite wonderful once you let yourself be a part of it. It's on your side, you know? And these rules and systems of contracts and working for money to pay for a house you don't have time to be in anyway is like building a boat and trying to sail on concrete. You need to go back to where you belong, and that is a place you need to find yourself. Don't settle for the town where you grew up or got a job, because somewhere out there a place exists where things work in harmony with your very heartbeat. And that's where you will find flow, balance, possibilities.

Freedom.

Well, at least this is what I told myself every day as I fell asleep with the fire still burning and the moon shining high up in the sky and my head spinning comforting from two bottles of wine, and I smiled with tears in my eyes because it was beautiful and so god damn sad and I did not know how to be one of those without the other.

Home

Your relationship with the places you live will be the most complex and informal connection you will ever have, and never figure out. It will be closer to you than your own mom and dad, and yet more unfamiliar than a stranger on the street. The places you will wake up in, the couches you will fall asleep on. The streets you will wander during afternoons in October when the autumn cleans the air pure and fresh, and the town is coloured in all kinds of beautiful, yet all kinds of sadness. The cities you will try to call your home, but never quite will, for your relationship with your home will be the most tangled up and complicated form of love you will ever know, and you will never want to untangle anything more than just the concept of simply being home. The many times you will put down your suitcase, stand in the middle of another empty room and slowly echo back a whisper of "let's call this home."
For a while, at least. Like love.

There will be countries or seasons where you will feel safe and calm, which might show itself as a small feeling of just home. But you will see, as the spring slowly blooms once more, that if you stay curious and interested, in this and that, in everything there is to be interested in, you will wake up one day and once more stand in the middle of that room, pick up your bag and slowly echo "it's time to go".

So now it's September and I'm lying on my back in yet another hostel somewhere far up north. I have places to go and things to be and I think I've spent more time thinking about home, and where I might find it, than I've ever felt it, and I'm thinking that I'm not a kid anymore. I'm growing older on this road I've built by myself, and it might be time to simply shift the mindset. To give in and not conquer. To simply, and as hard as it is, realise that for people like me, and maybe you, there will never be one static definition that you can point at and say "home". For I find myself more at home wherever there is anything interesting to see or feel or be or learn, than I ever will in a place of "having," anything or everything, for belongings will be lost or sold, broken or a burden, and you should try it; leave a suitcase of your things by the bus station, because it's just too much to carry, and you should try it; the freeing feeling of lightness. Simplicity. Nothing to lose.

So, to my untangled conclusion: here I am, far up north, wide awake as the clock strikes moon. 12 months of trying to build a home behind four walls and paid dues; I'm back up, packed up on the road, and I've never felt more at home.

Whatever that means.

The Sweetest Rain

This morning I woke up to the sound of white rain
shattering on my window.
The raindrops kept falling like the sweetest music
leaving tears on the glass,
which is what music does to me,
most of the time,
but silence too. and rain.

I'm living with your letter and I'm growing a ritual in reading one
line every morning,
or every time I think I'm forgetting you,
and I'm still not sure why I do that because there's nothing more I
wish for than to forget you.
To erase you from my daily habits and not see you in everything I
do.
To not feel your hands on my skin
in the morning
and not hear your words
at night
but still I cling to what you gave me
and taught me,
made me,
and I am still sorry.

So I woke up early to the sound of rain and bought an umbrella by
the man at the corner next to the coffee shop.
But there was a homeless man
on the other side of the street
and he seemed sad too,

sadder than me,
so I gave him my umbrella because he didn't have one
and he smiled at me
with realness in his eyes
like you used to do
and I'd forgotten what that felt like,
looked like,
and it was nice to feel appreciated again,
for a while.

There was a lonely bartender last night
and I told him stories about the sound of train stations
where no train arrives,
but he must have thought me lonelier than him
because he kept saying "drinks on me"
and I would never argue with someone who spends his days pouring
drinks to wandering souls, eager to find someone who might listen
and might not care
but that's not the point
and at least he seemed to enjoy the company
of me
because he smiled and answered and told me things too
and it was nice to just sit there and enjoy the simple pleasure of a
conversation,
with someone I didn't know, because I like the way strangers look at
me.
They make me sure, of myself and other things, and I speak freer
and louder and I don't try to hide my excitement for life
or sadness because of love
and I haven't made any mistakes yet, for them,
to them,
or in the life I wish to live.

Anyway,
I'm living with your letter and there was a lonely bartender last night
and I might or might not have shown it to him
and he might or might not have thought it was fiction
because by the end of another drink he said he'd read my book
and if I knew I wouldn't have told him
my stories
or showed him
my letter
because I wish for strangers and clean slates
and this god damn bartender knew every single piece of identity I
ever had
and so I asked for another drink and he kept saying "drinks on me"
and we didn't stop until we both had forgotten about the lack of our
strangeness
and I wish to find a way to strangeness even in the morning
when the spinning has stops.

But there is no strangeness.
Only the sound of white rain
playing sweet music on my window,
leaving tears on the glass,
which is what music does to me
most of the time
but silence too. and rain.
and I guess that's enough for now.
Until the smell of you vanishes from my skin,
that will be enough for now.

I HATE TO SAY THEY TOLD ME SO

I keep my windows wide open, falling asleep to the sound of a lonely car somewhere far away, a bit outside of Berlin where I live now. And there are cracks in the roads here,
because no one cares to fix things up
this far out,
and because there are better things to do.
Like the way I'm thinking that maybe you and I weren't that much of a mess; weren't really such a long fall, like I felt it was. Maybe we just finally realised that there are so many other things to do, better things to do, than fix the cracks in the roads that will only keep on cracking,
because it's too far out and people don't drive here very often anyway.

I'm sorry for the absence. Sorry for the metaphors. I know you never liked them and my poetry was never understood
but still I kept on writing, mentioning you in every line because I thought that maybe one night you will read it. And then maybe you will realise what you're doing to me, with me, for me, and maybe then we can find a new way. A better way. Another way.
But you kept growing colder and I kept growing smaller, and now I'm sleeping with the windows wide open, falling asleep a few minutes before it's time to get up, a bit outside of Berlin where I live now. And I'll keep writing metaphors like cracks in the roads because that's what I do and that's important to hold on to, I believe, and I need to hold on to myself, I've been told, because I belonged to you for so long, for a while, but not anymore.

So I will hold on to the metaphors. But know that they're all still metaphors for you and I and us: a question I never figured out.

JUST ANOTHER DAY
Berlin

There are moments when I'm exactly where I want to be.
There are days, like today, when I'm just as happy as I always knew I could be.

People keep asking what I do for a living and I keep answering that I don't believe in making a living. That it's a concept that has been twisted. I tell them I believe in making a life and money is a distracting object if there's anything left at the end of the day, and I just want to go on well. Make it through the day. So I smile and raise my glass and they laugh and take my hand, saying "here's to the youth," pointing at me. And I might just be young
and naive
for I still believe in the freedom of choice
of how to spend your life.
So they toast to the youth, who still thinks she's free,
and that's all fine by me.

Today was a great writing day and on great writing days nothing can bother me. The way my world feels balanced when I can create something out of nothingness.
Wait, let me take it from the beginning:
I woke up to a grey sky and I was gloomy and worried, like I often am, and I never sleep very well for I dream of him and them and all the rest and it's cold at this time of year but still I wake up sweating, heart pounding, chest aching.
It's been a quiet month and my voice is untrained and weak

40

from late nights. Cold air and strong drinks.
But there are some days that every artist dreams of, when it's all in
the right place and the chords sound right and the melodies grow in
the air all around. The words come fast and it doesn't take much, a
few minutes, closed eyes, silent mind – and it's there.

So some mornings I wake up and things feel wrong but are right and
it's been a silent month for I don't sing very much
but this morning I wrote and sang and created something
from nothingness
and it put my very self in balance.
My body into being.

Anyway,
I wrote my song and took my walk and made my way to the bar to
celebrate myself for feeling fine and usually people are quiet there,
take my order and let me be. But today I felt fine and not strange
or sad
and the town was not busy so the bartender had time
I think
for he asked where I was from and what I did here
because I spoke English
and not German
and so that's that.
I said I was just passing by,
on my way
to somewhere else
and he asked to where
and I said anywhere
and he smiled
and it was nice.

Nice because I was honest, which I rarely am, and he was nice,
which people rarely are, and after a few drinks he brought another
one
"on the house"
and sat down and asked what I was writing.
So I showed him
and he smiled
and we talked Bukowski and Woolf, Thoreau against Emerson
and it was beautiful.
The way the time passed by and chains fell down and I felt okay,
which is rare these days,
but I did
and I still do
as I sit on the floor in an empty room
with friends I've met on my way,
and they've told me to put stuff on the walls and decorate the hall,
but I've said this isn't permanent,
and neither am I,
and if I change fast enough I might be able to write another song
soon enough because it's all in the movement. All in the waves. All
in the change.

So anyway,
it was a great day and nothing in particular happened. Nothing to
make the books or the papers or the headlines,
but it was sincere,
and I felt okay
and that's rare those days.
And it's moments like these that I know I will be okay
for it will all make sense
one day
because I'm still on my way.
I'm going somewhere

and that's the whole point.

I'm still on my way.
And that's the whole point.

(If you see the boy in the bar
tell him I bought the book he talked about
and learned the song he sang
and that I found my way
home
wherever that is.
Tell him he's got a beautiful mind
and a beautiful smile
and that's rare these days.)

We're all on our ways.
       And that's the whole point.

The Becoming (#2)

I died several times
that month.
In the cold,
in the snow,
on my way home.
It starts slowly.
Something growing in your chest,
like an emptiness that takes up space,
too much
space,
and you press your right hand to your heart
to comfort
and shelter,
but the heart ponders on,
or not,
and mine kind of did,
unwillingly,
and that's why it hurt.

I passed the church every morning on my way home
and one day I'd had enough.
I opened the big, heavy door with a creak
and walked on my toes
like you do in cathedrals
looking up,
as if the spirits were watching
observing
and would wake up.
It was one of those churches that make you hold your breath

with a glorious ceiling
and sculptures
and scriptures
and people forever resting on the walls
and I've never been religious or prayed and never will
but I needed salvation and forgiveness, and I've heard that people go
to church to find these things.
To be freed from sins,
so that's where I went.

I told the priest I had loved and lost and couldn't breathe for my
throat got too tight and I think he saw in my eyes that it was real.
That my pain was real,
for he didn't question
or shake his head,
just listened with all eyes on me
and I'm not sure what I was expecting
but the priest just took my hand and said
"you'll be alright, kid."
We stood there for a while, me not knowing how to tell him that I
won't, wouldn't, don't know how to be
alright,
so I slowly asked what to do
with a voice thin enough to slip
and he said
"go love and lose and hurt some more"
and I didn't know what to do with that so I left.

Church didn't help me
so I took a bus to a place with no clocks
or computers
or anything else
for that matter

45

except for a room high up on a hill where people sat cross legged on the ground
to still their minds.
To not do or be or feel
anything than what is.
So there I sat for six days straight and I did not eat
and barely slept
for I'd had enough and I needed salvation
and they told me meditation would do it.

A fast-taught meditator
they called me,
but I think I missed the point
because when I left the place with no computers
or anything at all
my mind was back to a blur
and my heart
was still in pain
and I kept meditating by myself
every morning like a priest in pain
but it did not help.
I was still
in pain.

I joined a running team
because I'm a good runner
and they told me I had the will to fight
and fight I did.
I was dedicated like a sinner in the rain, more than the others,
and I ran and ran and ran and ran
and on Sunday morning with the rain pouring down
while the rest stayed in bed
I ran my races, faster every week,

with the rain drops falling down my face
or tears down my cheek
or maybe both,
but fight I did
until my legs were sore and my mind was too
and I could sleep for a whole day straight.

But no matter how fast I ran
or how many hours I fought
my heart just kept on troubling,
trembling,
and it seems to me that no matter how many miles I will run
I will never run from myself,
or my heart,
or my thoughts,
for they follow
and you just end up running into yourself.
So after a three-hour long run a Monday morning I told the coach I
had to quit
because I thought Monday was a good day to leave and start anew
and that's what I always do
so leave I did.

Running didn't help and church didn't help and meditation didn't
help either
so I made it to the bar
where I always seem to end up,
and it feels like they know me there
no matter where I am.
So there I sat, alone at times and not so alone at other times,
but it was nice, for a while, to just sit down
and the whisky might have helped
but there is a sense of acceptance going on in a place like that.

Like people have stopped thriving, striving, settled in to a quiet existence
and no one demands anything.
No one expects anything, or hopes, or has dreams,
and if they do, they do it full out
like castles in the sky and mystical forests.
Endless oceans of ships and love.

So I died many times that year.
In the cold, in the storm, on the run or on the drunk
for my heart did not want to beat
but kept on beating anyway
and my pain was as real as real can be,
and I tried to learn and deal and run and feel
but nothing really worked.

I built a comfortable home in my sorrow and settled into a quiet living. No sparks or grand gestures, just a simple daily hymn to comfort. The leaves fell off the trees and coloured this city in all kinds of pretty, and some days that was enough to make me smile at least a little bit, within.

I can't quite recall how, when or why, but the passage of time really does heal what seems impossible to heal. The daily task of getting by adds up to weeks and months, and you will find yourself a little more at ease one day, some days, if you just keep going. Keep doing, keep being. One day, when the spring wakes up and the air is crisp, you will catch yourself smiling, thinking "that felt good," and you will laugh again, suddenly more often than not, and one day, though far from here, you will say things like "grateful" and "content", and maybe even "I'm happy".

I think it's something in the letting go. How I simply stopped aiming at that point at the end of the finger and took a step back. We're striving and thriving, always wanting something more, but take a short second and just look around you. All the wonderful things you actually already have, and are, and see—right now.

I let my eyes see what was simply in front of me, instead of trying to find that spot somewhere far away, where I thought I should be. There was the sun, there was the city, the people, and in the middle: me. Still here. Still doing. Still okay. So my point is: You still are. I still am. *So we're doing just fine.*

Sometimes, there is no other salvation than to just keep doing. Sometimes, the only trick is to simply keep breathing. And with the small amount of wisdom I hold today: I promise you, one day you will thank yourself for simply holding on. One day, though far from here, you will find yourself walking light and sure and fine again, despite of it all. And one day, though far from here, you will catch yourself saying things like "happy" and "how nice," despite of it all. One day, you will meet someone again who will make your heart beat in all kinds of weird rhythms. And one day, you will have strength enough to go to new places, learn new words and understand new opinions, again, and that day you will thank yourself for simply holding on.

You want to still be here for that day.

It was April and the sun stood high and I was thinking things like "exciting" and "lovely," despite of it all. I didn't throw thoughts back to all things past, like I always thought I would be, from now on, and the months to come would be the discovery of the world all over again. The discovery of me, of how much this heart of mine is capable to be and feel and love and grow, and dear me;

dear, tired little heart;

thank you. Thank you for holding on.

I wouldn't want to miss this for the world.

ALBUM JOURNALS

Learning What It Means To Be An Artist.

———————————————

These are journals and thoughts that I kept to capture and record the
whole journey of writing and releasing my album
"I Must Be Gone and Live, or Stay and Die".
Writing these letters to myself and about myself, became my way to
reason and make sense of what I was trying to create. I lived solitary
and not many people understood what I tried to achieve, so I kept to
myself—kept those journals to myself—until now.

(The album was released October 2014)

Why I write?
Because it hurts not to.

The Artist's Way

It was a long day in the studio and I couldn't make my voice sound right. It was the atmosphere. It was the time of day. The time of year. It was too much light because the world was awake and I can't seem to function when it is because it blurs my head. Fills it with clutter and useless thoughts about what others will do today, tomorrow, every week and all their lives and they all seem to do so many things that I just don't and it steals my focus.

My focus. I must focus on my work. The only thing I have and want to have and I must not slip. Must not pull the steering wheel.

So it was too much light but then there was the lack of light because it's winter and Berlin has never felt so empty. It takes effort and energy just to make my way from the door to the bus and if I were like every other soul I would stay in, too, with friends and warm drinks and no hustle. But I'm not

like other people

so I make may way to the streets every day. I need the space. Need the air. I'm like an animal in a zoo and I'm easily observed through screens and words, but lately I've pulled the curtains early every night and I let them hang until late in the afternoon, and lately I've been thinking about the sages. The Stoics and the hero's journey, the ones I admire and the ones I watch and read and study

and not one of them spend their days pleasing other people's definition of success, and neither should I, but I feel them. Eyes in the back, expectations all around, of my beliefs and dreams and hopes;

the pressure of time.

So it was a long day in the studio and I couldn't make my voice sound right. It was the time of year and place of sound and lack of light and I do have things I want to say and sing and write on the walls of this broken town but I don't know how to. Misinterpretation is a sin I can't live with so I stay away.

By the time the streetlights lit up I called it a day and took down the microphone. Shut the monitors off and made my way home, which I often call these roads, because I've spent more times following streetlights and rivers than I've spent inside four walls and they call me crazy, stubborn, to keep walking in those worn out sneakers when it's minus 15 and there's ice on the river, but I'd rather be cold and alive than warm and in chains and so I walk.

The craftsmen make it seem so simple. The writer presents his words as if they came as natural as a breath. I put my headphones in and the songs with the sounds and atmospheric layers spread wide as if it just happened out of natural euphoria in the flick of a second and this is the danger with art. The art is not the art-form itself, but the way the artist makes something complicated feel uncomplicated. Something messy feel intact, something weak feel beautiful and this is the danger. Because I am not intact, but messy, and I write with the storms like a hurricane, grabbing everything my fists can fill and throw it on the paper and sing until my voice is soar with no technique and I am not intact. I catch my breath and sober up, the day appears and the world wakes up and so I stand, tilting my head to observe what I just did, what just happened, and I see no trace of art. No trace of simplicity, or love, or beauty, like they all want, and I want it too but it's not that simple. I tilt my head to the other side to make sense of the dark spilled ink and uncontrolled melodies and the guitar is out of tune and I am not intact. I have paint on my hands, I broke another nail and I glued my chair together with my own hands because I just need somewhere to sit and if I sit down softly it still carries me well.

But I've practiced my skill, sharpened my knife. I was young and not yet living when I made a deal with the lord to give myself to my call, and I do not back down. So I turn away from the spell of the night, warmer clothes, put on the coffee and wash myself up. I undraw the curtains, open the window with the pure air cleaning my lungs, and I start to pick up the pieces. The pieces I produce on the floor every night but I don't know how or why, until the day appears and I sober up. I observe them like a puzzle. Find entrances and exits as if I read a map of my very own soul, and just in time for the waving of the sun I start to see a pattern, a logic in the mess, and this is where it starts.

I am 23 and I am learning what it means to be an artist, for I am not an artist, because it takes life and a life lived well, to the limit, to see the patterns in storms, but I am 23 and I am learning. I am learning shame and solitude, forgiveness and goodbyes. I'm learning persistence and the closing of doors, the way the seasons come and go as I keep walking on these roads, back and forth, to find myself in new time zones, new arms with new phrases and new goals. And it hurts to become, hurts to find out about the poverty and gaps, the widow and the leavers. It hurts to accept that it hurts and it hurts to learn how easy it is for people to not need other people. Or how easy it is to need other people but that you can never build a home in someone's arms because they will let go one day, and you must build your own.

There are times when I doubt being an artist. When I slip back down on the floor and sigh high to myself because it all seems too hard. I collect my heroes on my walls and I think to myself that maybe I'm not one of them after all. I press my ear to the ground, hearing laughter from below and I wonder how I will be able to create something beautiful when my focus goes to the simple act of breathing, which is not so simple, for me, because it takes a lot to wake up and face myself in the mirror. Make my way to the streets of this town and just keep going, because the simple thing would be to stay inside, safe, behind closed doors.

But see, I'm coming to the conclusion that that's the whole point. That is the act of the arts. It is not the task of writing about the simple ride from bus to town, but the ride that was not so simple, not so joyful, but to make it feel okay anyway. Because life is not so simple most of the days, but it's okay anyway, because we're all on the same ride, all in the same boat, but not everyone can make it feel okay, anyway, and that is the job for the artist. That is why we exist.

A place that must be filled.

So I stay on the floor, with my ear pressed hard to the ground for a while. Memorising the sound of laughter and lightweight steps of a child, the way they soon will grow up and see and feel and realise that the bus to town is not always that simple, but pretty hard most days, but I want them to know that that is okay, anyway, and I am the artist and so it is my task, my mission, my purpose, to make these kids know that things are okay even when they don't think they are, and I still have time. Still have time to learn how to tell them, sing to them, write to them, but I have not a second to waste.

So I sit up and brace myself. Lock my eyes on the blank canvas on the wall, in my mind, in my chest,

and start to paint.

It was a long day in the studio and I couldn't make my voice sound right. It was a long way home and the bus was slow and the snow kept falling and the wheels kept spinning and it was a long day, leading to the night of time and place where it all became the pattern I'd lost, the trace of steps and balance of composure and sometimes it takes a year or two to make it all tie back up and this is the artist's journey. This is the artist's way. The pattern-less walk through the woods to learn how to build his map on his own.

There is beauty even in the ugliest mess,

and it's the artist's job to find it.

Journal II
MMXIII

So I left and found a new name; started to pave my way. I was strong and fearless but scared and sad, though only within, and no one knew because my skin was so much thicker back then. My walls were not yet fallen, like years do to you, love does to you, and I was a soldier. I soldiered on.

I have no regrets because I let life happen. I can stand up on my own two feet and proudly say that I embraced everything that came my way and I did not turn around. I soldiered on. Even when my heart broke, when my ankles ached, when my knees locked—I kept going. To God knows where, but there I went and if there is one belief close to religion I've held tight to my whole damned life it is that as long as you don't stop you have no yet failed. So kept going I did, and I still do and keep going I will.

Life did not impress me and I did not impress life. We were two companions who'd been forced together, and we tried to get a long or coexist but communication failed and I was misunderstood, and misunderstood life; until I found art. Or art found me, which it rather feels like because I never sought it, never wished for it, it just showed up one night when I needed it the most and it communicated in a way I finally understood. It spoke to me, sang to me, danced for me, and for the first time I understood and could make myself understood, and that's when it all changed.

I turned myself into an artist because then my life would be about creating meaning out of ugliness and that would be my life, and it was noble. It was the beginning of a journey, the creating of the world every single day and I was not bored. I was ecstasy and creation and nothingness turned into melodies and I was dancing with the spirits.

For a while, at least. But then the days went by and I had my fun. Conquered the hurdles and climbed my mountains. Embraced my life and all it came to be about,

and now I find myself wandering empty streets in Berlin on Christmas Eve

by myself

and I am not impressed.

I am unimpressed by myself and all around because I imagined myself great by now. Shaped and built to the limit of my own capacity and I had vast dreams and plans and I was ready to act on them, and so I did, but I am not

great

but unimpressed.

I keep wandering to new places to feed my eyes with new views, new voices, new stories, but nothing sparks the fire and I'm bored.

There's been a lot of pressure lately. People counting on me. Believing that what I write is all there is and forgetting that I am not poetry and beautifully written melodies,

but simply a scattered soul, using poetry to piece it back together. For look, in between the verses I'm still a mess, but they don't see that. Only the finished song. The produced record. Edited. Mixed. Mastered even.

See,

I am not a finished poem and I am not the song you've turned me into. I am a detached human being making my way in a world that is constantly trying to push me aside, and you who send me letters and emails and beautiful gifts wouldn't even recognise me if you saw me walking down the street where I live tomorrow

for I am not a poem.
I am tired and worn out and the eyes you would see would not be painted or inspired
but empty and weary
from drinking too much
at all times
and I am not the life of your party who sings and has glorious words to speak
for I don't speak much
at all
and my voice is raspy and unsteady from unhealthy living and not much sleep and I only use it when I sing and I always sing too much or not at all
and never when people are around because they expect poems and symphonies and I am not
a poem
but an elegy
at my best
but unedited and uncut and not a lot of people want to work with me because there's only so much you can do with an audio take, with the plug-ins and EQs and I was born distorted, disordered, and I'm pretty fine with that,
but others are not.

So how do I do this? How do you do this?
For I have vast visions not yet achieved, the reasons for my existence,
but I fear I need to do some cleaning out of closets.
I need to throw out and reassess. What to keep or throw away
and I've built this life on zero budget but a hell of a lot of will
and it did me well. To not have any options. No alternatives.

I was born to hustle to just get by and I must stop cursing my place
and will to survive, for it shaped me. I need to get rid of the layer of
pressure to seek the space, and time, to simply be amazed, again.
Oceans. Conversations. Music I never liked but could learn to, if I
try, and I must learn to feel
the simple pleasure of being alive
again.
I must turn away from the spectators to come back to love.
I don't want to be a critic of the world, like I am now;

      I want to encourage it.

03.00

Am I making something worth while?
I'm not sure.
I write and I sing and I hear words from time to time about my life
and choices making ways, into other lives, other hearts,
but am I making something worth while?
I'm not sure.

There was a boy last night who I never spoke to because I was too
drunk and still shy, but mostly lonely, and I couldn't find anything
lightly to say,
so I simply walked away.
But still wondered what he did with his life
because he didn't even speak to me
or look at me
but still made me wonder who he was
and I walked away asking
Am I making something worth while?
I am not sure.

I am a complicated person with a simple life
and I am the reason for everything that ever happened to me.

Dream, Fight, Achieve

Lately I've been doubting, thinking and questioning. Loving, crying, walking, running; not sleeping, drinking, laughing, doubting some more, thinking some more
and this morning I bought a new notebook and wrote a new plan. I admitted new aims and wrote new goals.
Today I imagined my biggest dreams, of where to be in a year and two
and I did not scale it down.
I did not scale myself.
Who I am. What I am. Where I live, with whom I live
and what I have to do to get there.
Today I planned my next move, my next project and my next adventure. Things I dream of doing that no one knew I ever would
and you might say "you can never do that" and I will smile and say "watch me"
and today I dreamed
about things you might say
"no, you can't do that"
for I haven't been dreaming in a long time,
because people stole them from me,
too many times,
but today I did dream,
and I flew.
I dreamed of music and poetry, words and worlds. Love and wars, both inner and outer and I dreamed of people and places. How to lose and how to gain
and I dreamed of hurt and happiness. Of home and of strangers, empty streets and crowds from stages.
Trains at night and old books from foreign book shops. New songs

sung from higher grounds and my words printed between thicker
covers
and I flew.
I flew
and I will not come down.
And you might say "no, you will never do that, that's not you, not
who I know, not who I thought you were"
and I will say
"watch me,"
for I never did this to fit in
or stand out
but to live.
I started this in order to live.
Live a life I'm proud of. Excited about. That's worth writing about.
I wasn't born to be a skeleton
and I was not born to shrink.

I came to beat the odds.
I came to grow,
and I don't want to fight to shrink
anymore.
I want to grow
bigger,
not smaller,
and I want to grow.

I'd rather burn in flames than fade away.
  I'd rather burn in flames
    than fade away.

Write Like You're Obsessed

You must write like you're obsessed and possessed. You can't let the objectives of right and wrong hinder you from pushing through, and you must let the words flow like a storm you can't stop and don't look up until it's all over. Until you let your arm rest with a deep breath and feel relieved that you got all through. You kept up.

It will be messy. Chaotic. A beautiful catastrophe. The mental picture of an ordinary youth, living an ordinary life, in an ordinary town,

with an extraordinary mind.

Because see, your external circumstances will not matter if you see wider and further. You must be mad enough, strong enough, brave enough, to turn inwardly. Everything you'll ever need to create eternal passages of magic is already within your reach. Just close your eyes and trust.

You must write like you're obsessed.

You must be a myth that your lover can't grasp

and you must chase the moon like a wolf in the night, as if it will show you something only you can understand. Everything you do is a ritual that can mean something more and you must connect and create bonds with the spirits both outer and inner. Seek the strange and mysterious, otherworldly explanations for yourself and things around. There is always more. Always more.

Nothing is ordinary

if you trust it so

and you must make love to him like his touch is your salvation.

You must dare to love and lose and hear your heart break into a million little pieces, glitter like diamonds in the night. A thin, white dress and hair let down, and you are not scared. And don't run into

hiding when the rain hits us like planets shot down to see who wants
to survive
the most
for you want to
survive the most
and you must not hide from madness.
Embrace it and seek it like only you can understand it. Grasp it,
transform and make us of it,
and you will, in time, understand.
If you keep your mind wide open to the new and the wild and
unaccepted ideas that might not make sense, and that's why you
want them.

You must love and live and write like you're obsessed and possessed.
Go mad for what you believe in.

THE PROCESS

February, 2014

This journal, and what I discovered by writing it, formed the vision of what
I wanted my album "I Must Be Gone and Live, or Stay and Die" to mean
and be about. It shaped the way I wrote, recorded and released it, and the
journey of this album became the proudest journey of my life.

***

I will try to write this as clearly as I can and not involve my normal
sense of messy prose or rhyming rhythm for I'd like to practice what
I teach, even though it's hard, and I'm learning simplicity.

I've promised myself to approach the producing and mixing of this
new album in a different and more harmonic way than I've done in
the past. I'm looking back at my first album and I see an open
battlefield. It was messy and chaotic, the pieces didn't fit, and it
wasn't until weeks later, when it was finished and closed, that I dared
to listen to it from start to finish and realise that I did it. I got it
together, kind of. I am proud, kind of, but still hear the cracks and
feel the aches, the pieces that never fit and bolts that weren't meant
to be. But as I've come to the conclusion that this new album, this
book, this adventure, won't be about just creating another album, I
want to remember it differently.

This will not be about the finished product. The goal is not the
finished album that people will hold in their hands, or have on their
iPods. The goal is above and beyond that. It's about what I can
achieve inside the thick layer of skin, both my inner and other
people's inner. The physical product, like a recording, is just
something I'd like to use to get there. I want to reach hearts. Make a
mess inside someone's mind and leave a mark, a thought, a new

feeling they never had, and the physical album is just my tool to get there. The music is just a small part of the bigger picture, the bigger piece of the artwork called my story that I'd like to create.

This is about the IMPACT of the JOURNEY. When I will draw the timeline on my wall, wherever I will be by then, and visually draw where and who and what I was when I first put pen to paper and wrote the first song and the first chapter, and then where I will be when these songs, that book, finally reach the hands of someone else out there – that is the story.

The goal is not a finished recording, but how the process, the journey and the life of that recording or those words can impact someone inside. I want to make people think. I want to make them question, feel comfort and discomfort. I want to shelter and build up storms, and even if in a small unconscious way, I want this story to change how someone lives his daily life. Even if it's just 10 minutes on the bus on his way home. If I can make that bus ride the slightest bit memorable, I will be happy.

I grew up in Gothenburg, the second biggest city of Sweden. I grew up with nature. Close to the sea and close to forests, trees, open spaces and silence. I spent the summers by the coast, with beautiful sceneries, cliffs and small summer villages with peaceful people minding themselves. I was never really well with other kids and I was more than happy in my own company. Getting lost and found, following whatever path there was to follow, and I loved the unobserved freedom. Even younger, my family and I spent the summers on actual, real camping trips. Yep, that's right, kids, an actual tent with sleeping bags and camper stoves. We drove an old Swedish Volvo, bikes on the back and the tent in the baggage. We stayed at different camping places for a few nights each and then moved along, and I loved every second of it. I had the adventures of my life, on my own, every single day. Each night as we arrived at a new campsite, I took my bike and went off while the others put the tent up before they could notice that I had escaped. I avoided the open paths or well walked roads and instead sought the hidden places where I imagined that no one else had ever been. It took me to the most beautiful nature and scenery, and that was enough for me to feel at home. Of course, I didn't realise it then, or think about the difference, but these days of early youth shaped my sense of not having a home in a physical place, but in a state of mind. I learned to feel home whenever I felt at peace. Wherever I was. And my teens became about learning how to find that peace, again.

By this time I had not yet discovered music, but I was always writing, and write I did. I filled notebook after notebook with thoughts and dreams, opinions and moments, and I was happy to know that no one would ever read these things. I had no thought of a career of any kind within writing or music or art. I found peace in solitude, free in nature, not knowing where we'd go next or what day of week it was or why we did what we did. And it's this feeling I've been trying to cling to lately. It's this mind set I want to remember and reproduce.

I think there is something to be learned in the simple act of being and going, without a goal. We never do that anymore. I don't do that anymore. We're always going somewhere, on our ways to somewhere. To get a little more money, a little more respect, be more liked or more accomplished. We step out of the door in the morning with a clear goal of where we want the bus to take us and what to do when we get there, and if something comes in our way we get upset because how dare someone interrupt our day??

Unlearning ugly habits is hard, especially when you've been studying time management and productivity and the art of getting things done as effectively as possible, and I am one of those people. But art is not to be rushed, not this time, not my art on this journey, so lately I've been trying to unlearn and untame. I wake up early and step outside before my mind has time or energy to paint and make up where I want to go and I just go. I keep going, trying not to fall into habits of rushing or thinking ahead and I try not to plan where I want to end up. I try to simply make the most of what comes in my way and use whatever I will be given. And this is beautiful, but also a practice for so many other things. As I come home and sit down to write, record or produce, I try to cling to this. I used to know exactly how I wanted the recording to sound, become and be, but I want to unlearn the patterns.

So I sit down and close my eyes, take a deep breath and start creating without expectations. I take a note, find a sound, play a chord, and if my mind starts to wander and paint up the road of where it all will lead and sound like in the end, I take a U-turn to the opposite side and keep wandering. Because there's a journey in the process of everything every day that we miss by knowing where it all will lead, and everything is more profound, more exciting, if you don't know what the outcome will be, and actually don't even care because it's about the way there that matters.

It is about the way there that matters.

THE FALL

This poem eventually became the song "The Fall",
and also led me to find the title for the album.

I said
"I love you so much it's killing me"
and you kept saying sorry
so I stopped explaining
for it never made sense to you
what always did to me,
to let what you love
kill you
and never look back.

As Romeo is dying, Juliet says
"I am willing to die to remain by your side"
and love was never a static place of rest
but the last second of euphoria
while throwing yourself out from a 20 story window
to be able to say
"I flew before I hit the ground"
and it was glorious.

Don't be sorry.
The fall was beautiful, dear.
The crash was beautiful.

WRITING FROM THE ROAD

House Concert Tour, UK, 2014

It's nights like these I feel like a kite. On the run from something I can't remember, but still I keep on running, just in case.
They had a room with broken windows. "Out of order," they told me, then I got it for half the price.

I recall a long sequence of slowly getting closer. Your hands a bit less shy every time. You were scared and unsure and I enjoyed the simple pleasure of watching you figure it all out. I lost the value back then and things like forever don't mean a thing unless you're tied to chains.
Tell me what you want and I'll show you who you are.

The streets were empty as I made my way to the room with broken windows. Only a lonely bartender closing the town, picking up pieces of a youth who never cared to settle. He threw me a glance and a nod, like a small sign of saying "we're in the same boat," staying afloat while others pass by, and it was nice. A small gesture to throw some comfort. And now I lie on my back in another temporary bed, hearing sounds from another city through a broken window. I'm recalling words and names, touches slipped like razors on my skin, and they will forever soar. They say you don't know what you've got until it's gone, and it might just be the loneliness, eating my insides from afar,
but I will never love you as much as I do when you're gone.

You will never love me as much as you do
    when I'm gone.

I never know what I have
    until it's gone.

I MUST LEARN TO SETTLE IN THIS WORLD.

To find my feet wherever they stand and build my home where I'm at
for the moment.

This morning I took the early train to the seaside, where no one goes at this time of year, and I had the horizon all to myself. The quiet flow of the waves making their ways to nowhere at all, the way the sun rose and coloured the sky all pink and it was something about the pace, the way nothing hurried, tried to adjust or change but just simply followed their own rhythm and it all worked out. It all felt settled. Like I wish I could.

They say the lost ones seek the cities because there they can be alone but not lonely and I dare to say that the streets of London shaped my muscles, the way my eyes work and wander because the city taught me how to see. How to see the moon and not just the top of the finger pointing to it, which I always did before. The city taught me that a home is not where you rest your head, nothing permanent, and neither is it a city or a country or a friend. The city taught me how to leave and to be left and it taught me that it is possible for flowers to grow from the concrete because I've seen people flower and bloom during the worst of storms, because it's simply necessary. It's about survival. The necessary breaths to go on.

There are days when I feel like I've seen enough, done enough, felt enough. When I call my wandering days over and slowly accept the quiet life from here on. When the dreams of making waves are a vague memory and the songs I meant to sing feel more like a finished painting, something to just observe and hang on the wall from now on, to those who wish to observe it. But then the night falls and the morning rise and horizons are calling once again and I'm on my way. Forests fresh and pastures new. And most of the time I'm fine with this.

I'm learning to be fine with this.

So maybe that's what settling into this world means. To simply, and as hard as it is, just settle into your own way of living – your own pace, your own rhythm – and not think too much about it. Just wake up and let your legs wander where they need to wander no matter where that may lead and just simply trust your path. There is a difference between what you want and what you wish to want. What you'd like to do and what you wish you'd like to do. I'm learning to not wish, but just do.

TRUST YOUR STORY
April, 2014

This is how it works:

I am a free soul, singing my heart out by myself no matter where I go and I call strangers my friends because I learn things and find ways to fit them into my own world. I hear what people say, rearrange it, take away and tear apart until it finds value in my reality and there I make it work. I find spaces in between the cracks, cuts where it feels empty, and there I make it work.

But I am not a poem. I am not a song. I know hard work and determination because I live it. I know dry skin and empty pockets, aching muscles and repeated circles because that is what it takes to run a mile worth remembering. (That is what it takes to lead a life worth writing about.) You train, week in and week out, for months or years, teaching your body to work independently from your mind for that's what it takes. You push through the pain because that's what makes the pain come a little later every day and you run longer and faster until you can run without thinking that you have to stop before you even start. The miles add up, the steps add up, and somewhere along the process you no longer have to think about putting one foot in front of the other because your muscles have learned the movement. Memorised it with precision and it's in your blood now.

It's in your very blood.

So you practice like this, for weeks or months or years. Doing repeated circles with one hand and not with the other and there will be mornings you wake up and can't remember why you started the practice in the first place, because what does it all lead up to? There will be seasons when you go to sleep at night, dreaming of far off countries and new beginnings and nothing will ever feel so distant.

But then there are moments, certain seconds, minutes or days if you're lucky, when it all finally falls into place. You rearrange and experiment, understand and tear apart for years, until one day it all suddenly fits. You're in the right position between the moon and the earth and your movements flow as if your body was shaped to do this very thing. Singing, writing, running – no matter what your call it. Your mind doesn't question or yell, doubt or direct. Just feels still but sharp, and people around don't complain or tear apart,

but accept and listen and take it as it is. It will feel like explosions and clarity, calmness and hurricanes and no matter what you feel – YOU ARE what is happening, and the happening IS YOU. And these are the moments you live for. These are the moments you thrive and strive and breathe and fight for. And when you go to sleep that night you will know you're on the right path, for today your very being was aligned with the stars, and if you were not

on the right path

how could you have come this far?

I've been wandering this road, fighting my way into existence for years. I've been broke and broken, young and felt old, homeless and sheltered, and it's not until now – in the beginning of the final touches of my album – that I feel every force of the universe wishing me good luck. Telling me I'm on the right track. I've known, or wished, all those years, that I would one day get to see how the hurdles and set backs taught lessons to use one day. How they built my strength, my resilience, and I've wished to finally one day see how it all was meant to be.

And today, where I sit after another long day of becoming, I think I'm finally starting to see the patterns. The storyline. The way you can trace my every step like dots on a map and how it all led me here – doing the right thing, at the right time, in the right way. And if you take away any of the dots, any of the setbacks, lost ways or wrongs, the whole story falls apart. My story. The very thing that makes me who I am.

So in the middle of the practice – your practice – in the repeated months of nothing but back and forth, hold on for the day you will be in the right place, at the right time, for that will all mean more than any mile of ache or hurt or sweat,
and I promise it will be worth it.
Trust your story. It will lead you exactly where you're supposed to end up.

***

An artist must be passionately in love with his art.
Obsessed or possessed – go mad for what you believe in.

***

THE MAKING OF A RECORD
May, 2014

Making a record is like doing an open heart surgery, on yourself, while the whole world is watching. Even though most of the world doesn't care and wouldn't mind and can't care less – that is what it feels like. They point and say "there she walks" and I close the door and try not to care, try not to notice the words and thoughts and whispers from all over and nowhere, for I remember when things were different. When people didn't eat my words like wolves but just simply took them as they were
and things were free
and I was free.
but I am not free
anymore,
for there are people watching.
And I call some of them "very close friends" but still I can't decide my name and they don't know what to call me and I've moved too many times the last few years so the letters go missing and again there I walk, feeling fingers pointing loud saying "there she walks", and here I am. Still alive. Who would have guessed, right?

Making a record is an open heart surgery. You rip out every organ, every impression, every trace of character and lay it out on the floor. You rearrange, try to make sense, piece it together. Some days you wake up energised and motivated, and you find yourself saying things like "I've never felt this alive", and "now I will finally show them who I always knew I could be." But then there are other days you fall asleep, drunk and alone on the floor, and wake up without having slept at all and the songs sound empty and the open heart surgery is failing, blood is lacking and so are you. You look at the pieces on the floor and find yourself saying things like "I didn't know this part was so ugly…" and "how could I ever let someone see this…" You want to take your very own inner pieces and bury them far and deep so no one ever knows and you walk for miles to maybe not find your way back, but you always do for that is the thing.

Making a record is an open heart surgery and the heart is a strong muscle, can take more than we want to know, and maybe it beats a little out of rhythm from time to time but it always survives, most of the time, and it's tiring and you're exposed, to yourself and your friends and the world all around, but this is your chance to piece yourself back together. In a better way. In the way you want it to be. You can shape and rearrange and redesign and tear apart. Find cracks and fill them up with poetry and rhyme, and this is my chance to clean things up. Clean this up. Clean my past up.

Life is an open heart surgery, some years, these years, and this is my chance to make it right. Tear apart and fill the cracks. Make it fit and last and shine, so I don't ever have to run away from friends or things or dreams, alone in fear, ever again, like I've done, because of shame –maybe – but this is my chance to make things right.

It was a long day and my voice is sore and the words didn't fit or find their ways, but here I am. Closed door, feeling fingers pointing loud saying "she's in there," but I made it fit at last. The last song done and closed and saved, and here I am. Heart still beating. Back together. The cracks are filled, the wounds healed up, almost, and I'm still here.

My record is done.
I never thought I would get to say that again.

"What you get by achieving your goals is not as important as what you become by achieving your goals."
— Henry David Thoreau

I Want To Be Known For How Much I Live

I want to be known for how much I live.
I want to be known for how regretless and reckless
I threw my bag over my shoulder
and how they saw me walk away
to places no one ever knew
and
I want to be known for how much I live.

How much I move and feel and hurt and laugh
and I want to be known for things like
singing
and
writing
but most of all
belonging,
for I wish to make someone feel at home,
everywhere,
anywhere.
With me
or through me
but most of all
unknown to me,
because it's how I can make someone get through their own days,
on their own,
a little lighter,
a little easier,
a little more together,
that matters.

Just like music
and poetry
helps me.

and I don't think there's a limit
for how much we can live,
how great we can live,
and so it's all up to us.

I want to be known for how much I live.

Finding Your People

August 12, 2014

It's one week left until the first single of my new album will be out for the world to take and tear apart; the consequence of everything I came to see and feel, know and be this last year, and that's why I'm scared. I'm scared because I want to reach people, make them feel and relate and know that they are not alone in anything because I am here and I hear you and I've felt it too. Just like those songs by those bands that I listen to let me know that I am not alone, and belonging is everything.

Belonging changes everything.

So I'm scared and nervous, because the aim to reach those rare and few people who will understand and listen are out there, I know it, but to get to them I need to pass thousands of others. Thousands of others who won't understand. Who won't relate or feel or like what I say and what I do or who I am,

and they are never too busy to let me know that they don't like what they hear or what they see or who I am

and so I'm scared. Because this album is not just an album to throw words on or dissect – it's everything I came to see and feel and know and be the last year, and that's why I'm scared.

So just stop, you might say. Just stop and turn around and keep your songs to yourself, and trust me, I've tried. I've gone away and turned my back and tried to escape

but see

I still remember being 16 years old and stumbling upon a song, a poem, a book or an album, and I remember sitting numb on the floor, holding my breath to not miss a single word, because he was speaking straight to me. He was singing straight to me as if to tell me that he understood and I was not alone. And I remember thinking "there are more people like me out there!" and that changed everything. I found my people. My family.

Belonging changes everything.

I remember buying my first guitar and playing until my fingers bled and my voice was sore because I had to know. I had to know if someone out there understood and could relate, to me and myself, and I thought that if I learned how to write clear enough, play well enough, sing loud enough, someone might hear and could let me know that

I

was not

alone.

So I practiced. Day and night, months into years, and one night I felt ready. I put it up online and then just sat there. The breath in my throat and heart beating hard and I was scared, but hopeful. Scared because what if no one got it? What if no one understood and my very heart would be dissected? Torn apart, never to be opened ever again.

But still I was hopeful,

because what if someone did understand. What if someone did see and felt what I saw and felt.

And that was stronger than the rest.

My hope was stronger than my fear.

So now, after a year of inwardly research, it's just a few weeks left until my album is out for the world to take and tear apart,

and I'm sitting on my floor with my notebooks and thoughts, guitar and beating heart

and I am scared

but hopeful.

Because maybe most of the people out there won't understand. Maybe most of them will throw ugly words about productions or mixing, or quality of sound, and maybe most of them will laugh or ignore

or tear my very heart apart.

But, maybe, someone out there will. Maybe someone will understand. Maybe I have finally learned to write clear enough, play well enough and sing loud enough to make someone's heart stop and beat at the same time, just like mine did and does, and maybe I can let that person know that he or she is not alone, just like that song that night let me know that I was not alone, and that saved me.

Belonging changes everything.

And that keeps me writing. That keeps me singing. Keeps me posting and publishing, releasing and emailing

and that keeps me

tweeting and blogging, and writing this letter

to you, tonight,

because the thought of touching one single soul out there is stronger than all the fear of those who won't understand,

and that keeps me writing.

So I am scared, but hopeful, because I know that I am not alone, and neither are you.

I MUST BE GONE AND LIVE, OR STAY AND DIE

The story behind the album.

I must be gone and live, or stay and die.
A line I have built my life on, in more ways than one, and a concept I find myself living according to over and over again. See, I am not one to settle for comfort and stability, warm blankets and chains to stay safe. I've found something I believe in so much that I'm dedicating my life to it, because I believe that this is what I came here to do. I'm learning how to act and walk, what to read and how to see in order to walk this quest, this pilgrim, this mission of becoming as much and as great as I possibly can be, personally, according to my own values, to suit the person I'd like to be.
I'm on a quest, and I'm walking it alone.

Since I packed my bag for the first time and stepped on that airplane, I have had my heart ripped to pieces by missing and goodbyes. I've been scared, worried, rejected and screamed at. Cursed the spirits or whatever kind of god there was. I've booked tickets back home, ready to surrender. I've begged my friends and loved ones to let me in, let me stay, take my hand and just let me rest. Be still. Please don't force me to walk out there again.
I have left and been left, stayed when I shouldn't have, and all I can say is this:
If you stay, you will just simply stay, and life is not meant to be a static place of rest. Life is supposed to be adrenaline and excitement, reckless love and hearts beating so fast you can hardly breathe. That's how I want to fill my life.
That's how I want to remember my life.
I'd rather burn up in flames
than fade away.

I'd rather burn up in flames
than fade away.

Life is way too vast and unexplored to stay where you already are.
You must leave to get somewhere new. You must take one step in
front of the other and keep walking. Even though your muscles
strain, even though your heart aches: you must keep going. To grow.
To learn. To be. This might mean leaving people or places, lovers or
jobs, but the reward is greater. The reward is life. Because if I decide
to stay, sit down and settle for comfort and safety, I will do nothing
but simply just stay. Stay as I am, where I am with what I am.

I'm not sure about a lot of things, but of this I am sure:
until the day I die, I will live. Live as much and as great and as vast as
I possibly can. Living recklessly will mean fear or anger, sadness or
pain, but I will not let it stop me. I will move forward because I
know for a fact that there are far more beautiful and magnificent
places, views, people and feelings in this world than there are dark
ones, and I know for a fact that we have no other mission in this life
than to be as great as we possibly can be, and there is no limit for
this. We can be far more unique than we want to believe, but
crossing that line to step over to extraordinary means pushing
through fear. Facing fear and discomfort, uncertainty and instability.
This might mean the uncertainty of not having a home. Financial
instability of leaving a job you don't like in order to find one you
love, ending a relationship that has bloomed and died, or moving
from a place that you have outgrown.

Being a person who pushes himself to his or her own limits in order
to become as great as he or she can possibly be means being a
person who is constantly faced with some kind of fear. May it be
mental or physical, may you be an athlete or a writer, YOU are

facing fear, every single day, by doing something your mind or body never did before. But by overcoming that fear you take one step higher on the ladder, and the goal is to take those steps every single day.

The higher you get,

the higher the fall will be,

and the bigger the fear of falling is,

but, rest my case,

the more breathtaking the view will be.

Small moments of clarity that makes up for everything.

The third song on my album is called "Heroes", and there is a middle part in this song that has been my own mantra many days of wandering along this path. The lyric goes:

"As long as I am moving, I'm right on the path I made."

See, you don't always have to know where you're going. You don't even have to know where you want to go or where you want to end up. Heck, actually it doesn't even matter because that is not, and has never been, the point. The point is that you simply ARE going. That you ARE moving. Because, as corny and cliché as the saying goes, the saying has survived because it simply is the truth: it is the journey that matters.

So

I must be gone and live, or stay and die

is not only a line from one of the most beautiful pieces of literature by one of the most unique writers the world has ever seen—William Shakespeare's *Romeo and Juliet*—it is also my life. How I left Sweden five years ago to go after my dream. How I left London and my own keys in order to wander the road for a year, to keep going after my dream. And it is how I left England and moved to Berlin one year ago, to once again keep going after my call. And I was scared, every single time, but I also knew that that was what I had to do in order to keep growing and moving forward. I must be gone and live, or stay and die.

So,

face your fear. Do what makes your heart beat faster. Go where you look over your shoulder because you simply don't know what's around you.

Embrace fear, because fear for me is the purest evidence of living wildly, loving deeply and going above and beyond what's expected of me. Everything I would like to stand for.

So go now. Go live. Grow. Learn. Be scared and be it often, and I promise you will reach heights you never thought existed.

I Write To Make Sense Of It All
2013–2015, Berlin

> *If I stay close to the sea,*
> *I will go on well.*

The violin player

There was a homeless man
on the street where I walked,
playing the violin
like nothing else would ever matter again.
It wasn't a very hard piece
or fast scales
but there was something in the way he just stood there,
playing note by note,
and I had to stop.
It was something about the way he just stood there
playing note by note,
sometimes the wrong one,
but he had his eyes closed
and holes in his shoes,
looking sad and tired
but hopeful and content,
and the notes kept singing
and people kept passing
but I just couldn't
for my world kind of stopped.

He played to survive,
(I think),
for the money (I think),
but still,
I don't think he cared.
For he had his eyes closed
and someone gave him money but he didn't notice

or look up,
just kept playing
note by note
as if his very life was strung to the strings.
As if he didn't know how they would sound
and each note was exciting,
each song something new.
An experience, like true joy
and not to be taken for granted.
A joy not to be taken for granted,
like I
always
do.

I walked home, feeling strange,
because I too make those notes come alive
every day,
but my eyes are not closed
but open
and each note is not an experience
but expectation
and if the music would stop one day,
if the notes wouldn't sound
or my voice wouldn't sing,
I think the homeless man
playing the violin
would find it exciting, to see what happens now,
while I would fall down hopeless
and angry
and curse my regrets
because I took it for granted,
what music does to me.

May I never take it for granted,
what music does to me.

I will never take it for granted,
what music does to me.

What loneliness teaches me

I know loneliness.
I know the smell of absence and the sound of laughter from the other side of the wall. The way you speak to yourself just to fill the lack of someone else. Anyone else. Anything else.
I know loneliness.

I move as often as I wake and I spend a lot of nights in cheap rented rooms, airports, or on a couch in a house of a friend to a friend's friend. Kind of. I'm no one's best friend and no one is my best friend and I'm not afraid to go to places all by myself. Like the town, or the sea, or the theatre. Actually, I love going to the theatre by myself. The things you notice when you're on your own, without anyone distracting you from the simple pleasure of noticing things. Like the way the old man is shifting his weight on the other side of the lobby. Bored and uncomfortable in those shiny black shoes I assume his wife bought for him, because they were going to the theatre after all. Or how the lady at the bar just bought her fifth cocktail, sitting straight in something I'd consider a way too expensive piece of clothing. I sweep the room and realise she's alone, just like me, and it hits me that we're not so different, that woman and I. Her 20 years more experience than me probably made the noticing a bit less exciting and so now she's seeking comfort in expensive drinks and dresses. I sit calmly in the corner with my spiked coffee, cluttering my notebook with sketches and words while observing these people, before I make my way into the theatre to lose myself in another world, another story, another universe, with no one beside me to draw me back to reality.

I like the way I notice these things, and how I wouldn't notice it if someone kept filling my mind with familiar words or conversations about subjects, because I seek the unfamiliar. How small, ordinary daily routines can turn into beautiful little memories. Like the way I spend every morning writing undistracted for an hour, just like I've done every single day for the last five years, but how a simple habit becomes exciting, new, unfamiliar, just because you're in a new town, with unfamiliar people to watch and hear and observe. In a coffee shop with strange cups and a new smell of their brew and the way that young boy seems sad but still relieved, and how I can simply sit in one place for hours and just be astonished, all my senses awake and sharp, and I smile even though I don't realize, because I'm just simply content in my own state of excitement. Excitement for all these small, seemingly familiar little routines, but for me it's all new. Like the way I spend the train-ride back home filling the last pages of my notebook with all new thoughts about small things unnoticeable to others, but astonishing to me. About how they live and how I live and who that boy was and why he doesn't want to go to school. And how the simple habit of writing music every night until I fall asleep becomes my safety, because that's what I know, that's what I do. But it's still unfamiliar, and the entering of new land every single night, because that song, that melody, these memories transform me into different worlds where all things are possible.

And you ask me why I enjoy my loneliness? Because loneliness doesn't have to be empty if you learn to see the possibilities it brings. Loneliness is not an empty space but more like a blank canvas. A blank page free for you to fill. With stories, possibilities and excitement. Or the simple stillness of watching the sun rise over the horizon in silence, in a foreign city. No one telling me about familiar things. The world is, after all, only our perception of it.

So I'm not afraid of loneliness, because it's teaching me.

They way I walk now

They way I walk now
you'd have a hard time recognising me,
on these streets
where I once imagined walking with you,
hand in hand,
like we always did.
And it never mattered where we were going
because it was all just fine.
I was always fine.
But they rest restlessly in my pockets now,
in a new town,
on these new streets,
and it's heavy to stay standing
for my body is half the size
when you're gone
and these buildings are tall and old and beautiful
and I wonder what secrets they hold.
How to stand so proud after so many years
because I'm still young but I feel worn
and I get through the days on too much caffeine and mood altering
chemicals
to stay awake long enough to make the poetry come alive.
I fall asleep on the floor with the music still playing
when my neighbour leaves for the office
and I'm jealous.
Because I wonder what it's like to go outside and know where to go.
Know where you want to end up
and just simply go there.
I've been making lists of things I want to do,

where to go
and who to be,
now that you're gone,
and it's nice and all
but,
it's just,
I'd rather write it with you,
and go there with you.
Be things
with you.

There were days when I still put on make up
in case you'd come back,
but I wear the same clothes and shower in the rain
and eat when I can and sleep when I can,
which is rare and not often,
so if you'd see me now
on these streets
where I once imagined walking with you
you'd have a hard time recognising me.
I takes a lot to run away.

The Ship

I feel like a ship floating in and out of my own life.
No regular consultation that tomorrow we'll reach the shore. That
there will be rest and food with drinks and a fire, for everyone to
warm themselves around, and in the morning we'll take off again. To
new lands with new hopes and you will always reach the shore and
no worries are needed, you're one of us here.
But instead I capsized my own boat and floated out at sea and it was
nice
for a while. It was quiet and peaceful and the surface of the water
made a lovely, dripping sound, and I spent nights lying on my back,
counting the stars and wondered where I was going.
But then I must have fallen asleep
because I'm waking up stranded on desert islands
and being alone is not fun when you're lonely
and suddenly you're the loneliest person on that whole damned
island and you can't find your boat. The peaceful quiet far out at sea
is suddenly the most terrifying silence you've ever heard and you
can't shut it up. The stillness turned into an emptiness that eats you
up and you can't decide if you're scared or sad or too tired to even
care.
So like this I drift, in and out of my own life,
like a refuge who never learned the skill of escaping for it wasn't my
fault,
I just wanted something to hold on to.
Someone to hold
on to.
A place to hold
on to,

and I have given my skills and talents and prayed to Gods and spirits
but they all keep telling me to keep wandering
and I keep screaming "to where??!!"
but they just smile
and so I keep going.
And if it wasn't for my own damned belief in a higher fate I would
have stopped and turned around many years ago
for my legs are tired and my head is too and I'm young but feel so
old
and I just wish for peace and warmth and nourishment of souls.

But my destiny tells me to keep going
so keep going I will,
and if there is something called a prisoner in my own life
that's what I am,
and I can't help but feel hopeless
but hopeful
because maybe this road will lead me somewhere I don't know
where yet, and it sparks a small fire of excitement.
Maybe one day I'll find the shore where they will welcome me and
say
"we've waited for you"
and I will smile and we will all be okay.

Maybe one day we will all be okay.

March 28, 2014

"Write a novel!" they say, "I want to read your novel!"
but how could I write a novel of hundreds of pages when all I want
to say is

    stay.

Journal III

I'm not sure as to where to go from here and I doubt there is a right
or wrong way, and so I'm back to talking to myself. It's been a long
year and I've been more than one in more than one way,
like a merry go round, chasing my own tale,
and I'm finally back in my own skin.

Have you ever felt it?
I woke up and nothing was particularly dark,
but I stabbed my own heart
from within
for I had skin to rip and shed.
I couldn't stand my very own self
and how do you do it then?
See,
this is the body I will live in and I have no choice.
These are my bones and this is my face and these are my hands. I
can curse and reshape and starve for as long as I want, but see, this is
still my body and I can not shed it. Can not rip away the parts that
make me who I am, and so how do you do it?

I get stressed and worried, just tired from time to time,
because I'm building my own world here. Standing on my very own
ground. I have no promises to keep or commitments to please but
still, carrying your own world on your own shoulders gets heavy,
and I tend to grow small
when things get heavy,
and a small soul is a great weight
for people around
and so that's that.

Back to walking on my own.

I can't focus my thoughts and my mind runs from one wish to
another, hoping to express, or make the best of each and every thing
I wish to say and scream and need
because my heart is full
but still empty
for I can not focus my thoughts
or words
and it's never dark around here.
It's June and it's youth and I never sleep
so my veins are getting clearer
and skin paler
and I'm alive but still a mess
and how do you do this?
When there are places to go,
and people to see,
but I'm back to growing small.

There are places to go
and people to see
but I'm back to growing small.

Essay: The City

"The mountains are calling and I must go."
– John Muir

But the city doesn't do for me what it does for other people. I remember the look in the eyes of people when I told them I lived in London. Like just the name was filled with promises of hope and luck and endless nights with strangers. But that was never the thing that made it for me. I lived in Bristol, the lovely little town in England that I forever will remember as sunny days by the harbour, long runs to Bath and back, and summer nights in the park. People ask me where I live now and I hesitantly say Berlin and already know what will come after. People blur out words about big city life, streetlights and endless opportunities. "Sure, it's great," I smile. Nod and say "yeah, yeah, it's nice," but the city never did for me what it does for other people. See, I seek the city because there is nothing sweeter than not being alone in your loneliness.

I seek the city
because there is nothing sweeter than not being alone in your loneliness.

Everywhere I've lived, I've found a small little room a bit outside of the city, where the cars are driving slower. Where there's only one local market where old men sell fresh vegetables on Sunday mornings, and where they remember my face. I make my way into the city at dawn, watching the people sleep-walk to the office somewhere far up in a building, where they stay the whole day until it's time to go home, and at the same time I make my way back to my side of town. Where the streets are empty and air purer. Where people talk a little lower and the cars are driving slower in order to not make too much noise.

103

So now I live a bit outside of Berlin, by a river which is beautifully sheltered by a thin layer of fog every morning. I run there, along the river, every day before the world is awake. Leading me through forests and pathless fields, small villages and finally out to Wannsee where the air is pure and the wind is not cold but free. My legs can stretch without touching anyone else.

Of course, I never tell this to anyone. See, the youth of the cities are of a special kind. The kind that just stare and go on, and they look strangely at me when I say that I don't have a phone. They ask how I have time to run for two hours every day and they can't understand how I only have one bag of belongings. They don't really care either for they have better things to do. But still I wonder how some people can do without it. Do without this. The stillness and quiet, and sure I love crowds too but only as a contrast. The way my mind would get swallowed up by fabrics and produced material if it didn't get the chance to wake up to the natural way the sun rises every morning. The clean air straight from the trees and the balanced way of noticing the seasons as they come and go, no matter what happens in or outside of my life. I wonder how anyone can fully appreciate the music without hearing the silent sound of a wave making its way to the land, a lonely bird sweeping through the air, or the powerful sound of a raw thunder storm in the middle of July, watching the rain pour down on the plants and flowers. And how the world feels cleaned up, pure and refreshed when the sun finally makes its way back again.

The nature will have its way and everything goes as it has to go and I wonder how anyone can do without it. The knowing of the real order. The system. Not the one the society built, of consumerism or bio-hacks, but the way nature shapes and recreates and flowers bloom and die, the seasons come and go and I am happy just to get to witness another sunrise, another moon. Fall asleep beside someone who understands, share another cup of coffee in the morning, or simply learn to be fine by myself. It makes it all feel ethereal. Infinite.

Sometimes I wonder what else anyone can ever ask for.

***

The more comfortable I get with being an artist,
calling myself an artist, the less I worry,
and the more I'm able to reach that place of pure,
true creative freedom.

***

A Coffee with Ray

I called in sick to work. Which isn't really work since the coffee shop can't really count as an office. But it felt good to have a ritual for cancelling all commitments for the day, and besides, maybe the guy who's bringing me an extra large coffee every morning at 8am sharp might have wondered, and we don't want that to happen, do we? Anyway, I called in sick, loafing around my apartment with an old acoustic record playing in the background. Drinking coffee and smoking cigarettes, wondering how to best make use of this cancelled day. The morning-sun filled my kitchen, highlighting the dust slowly drifting as an evil reminder. Maybe I should clean this place up, I thought to myself. Have one of those ordinary-people days with cleaning and laundry and all that stuff I never really did, because I considered it the way of nature, to let things have their way, and I liked it that way. An organised mess.

The record stopped. The house got quiet. The dust way too visible. I got dressed and made my way to my dear neighbour next door. An old gentleman in his 60s but still in his best years and with stories that only people like Ray can tell.

He was just making another pot of coffee as I opened the door without ringing first. He never comes to open anyway, just screams "I'm in the kitchen!" with that familiar and homey voice that only old people can have, like a collection of all the times they've already opened the door for people through the years. Spending time with older people is golden, and something everyone should take the time to do. It's something in the way they walk and smile and breathe, as if they have figured it all out. They're calm now.

I poured myself a coffee while Ray was tuning in his old school radio, one of those with a wheel you have to turn to find the right frequency. He sat down on the other side of the table, stirring his coffee but kept his kind eyes on me, smiling, waiting patiently on me as if he just had asked something. It's this thing we do. He doesn't have to ask me. He knows I will speak sooner or later and as the old man that he is, he was in no hurry to make it happen.

"I'm sad," I said without sounding sad. "And bored. So I called in sick, because I feel sick. Sick of myself."

"You called in sick to the coffee-shop?"

"Yes Ray, I called in sick, because that's what you do when you don't show up for your duties, no matter where your duties might be," I said, as if talking to my mom, when I was 13, which I kind of still felt like I did while talking to Ray. He just smiled, let me have my way because he knew I knew and we both knew that.

"So what are you gonna do about that?" he kept smiling, as if he was asking me the simplest question with an answer you should be able to work out through logic, like $1+1=2$.

"Well, I thought about leaving, or just going away for a while. You know, Jack Kerouac style. Maybe make a mission of it, like 'a year without technology in a cabin in the woods', and then write a novel about all the things I discover, like the secrets to living, and be named the next Henry David Thoreau and win the Walden Prize. Is there a Walden Prize, Ray? There should be, anyway, and if there's not, I can invent it. Yeah, so that's my plan."

He listened to me, amused, as if he was watching a child learning how to walk for the first time, stumbling and falling and getting back up again and again. "A cabin in the woods, huh?" "Yes, Ray, a cabin in the woods. Or maybe a trailer in the mountain, like *Into The Wild*-style, in Alaska?"

We sat there the whole afternoon, saying nothing in particular, even though I tried to tell myself I was serious, but I knew, and Ray knew, and we both knew that we knew and that's what's so great with dear old Ray. He knows stuff, you know?

New Hope

It's June and it's youth and I'm catching glances in the sky:
Tell me what you want and I'll tell you who you are.

It's the small moments of silence, in between our long undisturbed
moments of conversations, laughter and nonsense,
that makes it all matter.
Words never mean a thing if you don't know the lack
of them,
or sounds,
or laughter,
and so it's the small moments of silence I value the most.
You glance at me and I stare at the sky
like I always do
and it's June and it's youth and we're walking carelessly
like I haven't done in years.
But there was this one morning last month
or last week,
I can't remember,
when I woke up and I had actually slept
without dreaming
about things that ought to be forgotten
and I felt rested,
like I haven't felt in years,
and the sun was warm and nurturing and the air was crisp and not
dense and I felt lighter.
I heard laughter.

There was a lake where I used to live and I walked along the edge of
the water every day that year.

Every morning
for a year
and it cleansed me.
Gave me fresh slates and pure minds
and I needed it.
But I moved and the language is different here and it's tiring
most days,
to understand and make myself understood,
so the walks went awry for I stayed in bed
whole days
some days
and it took me five months to unpack my bag for I never changed
my clothes anyway and nothing else was needed.

But then there was this day the other month, or week, I can't
remember, when all felt pure and light and clean.
I woke up and sat on the floor in lotus, like I always do, but it wasn't
hard or heavy
but kind and light
and for the first time I made my way to the river
by which I live
and I walked by the edge of the water,
catching glances in the sky.
And now there is you and the moments in between the noise and
talks and the laughter
and it cleans out all the rest.

They say there are seasons for everything
and I'm glad the seasons come and go for with them
I come and go
to new places,
people and mindsets,

and this is how I live.

There's a season for everything
and everyone
and seasons come and go
and so do I
and eventually
most probably
you
but I'm glad it's just the blankness of the start
and I'm walking again.

It's June and it's youth and I'm catching glances in the sky.
Tell what you want and I'll tell you who you are.

Still Learning

I fall asleep at night thinking I did well and I feel well and tomorrow
will be a new day and we will get it right, we're on the right track.
But then I sleep and my mind curls up and I wake up in a haze.
Mind unsharp and blurred out
by dreams never remembered. I feel tired and unlight, and the places
I meant to go, dotted clear on my map, seem too far away and it
takes a lot to make it to the bus. Another day of nowhere to go but
still too many things I ought to do
and be
and see
and feel
and where is the time going anyway?
Because I remember this time last year,
where I was and what I felt, and I was sad and scared for I had
nothing.

Let me take that back.
Having nothing is a loose concept, not to be thrown around, because
possessions never gave me anything, but still I feel unstable.
See, this is the dilemma I never figured out and would like to clear
up:
I feel unstable when I have nothing to own or lose,
and I feel unstable with
anything…
something…
to own
or hold
and lose.

For I need to be free and feel free and know that nothing can bring
me down
and the only way to know that I can make it,
make THIS,
on my own,
no matter what, despite of it all,
is to know that I have nothing left to lose.

If I have nothing,
I have nothing to lose.
The philosophy I built my life on
but wish I never did.

I'm reading travel books and essays, watching *Into The Wild* on repeat
like a hypnotic song, humming me to sleep. Bukowski and *On The
Road*, Thoreau and leaving all being. Same old empty clichés, but still
I can't close the books, for I relate. Nomadic people writing about
location independent freedom and they all talk with grace and
certainty
as I sit here, writing prose and songs about the same damned things
but I am not
certain
but scared
for I know what I want and what to do and who to be but then
STOP.
        I am just a kid?
A child still in training, in need for guidance and mentors and no one
ever told me how to do this and that,
how to be this and that
so I had to figure it all out myself.
                I have to figure it all out myself.
I get it right from time to time but most of the time not
and these are the times I grow the most

and that's why I'm writing.

So I'm asking for just a little time to train my mind.
Train my mind to switch, throw off the weight,
to see uncertainty as curiosity.
Being scared as a sign of growing
and being broke as minimalism.
    .... ..
Minimalism... location independent...
I throw up on your labels and they're all just empty excuses for never
finding your place within society
and you can call it whatever the heck you want,
I am still me.
I curse labels and names more than the philosopher himself, and if
you want to call me a minimalist that's all fine
and if you want to call me a nomadic, go ahead
for I will go my own way
no matter what
but all I'm asking for is some time to train my mind
and accept what's been handed to me.

I am learning to feel safe within uncertainty
for this is the life I've built for myself
and I wouldn't change a thing
but still it takes practice.
Practice to see what you want to see, to shift your focus,
courage to stand up, after sitting down too comfortably too many
days,
strength to say yes when everything else seems to say no.

But I am learning,
and I am practicing,
and still,
still,
I have hope in who I am becoming,
for I still am, and that's more than I ever thought I would be by
now.

"Remember that very little is needed
to make a happy life."
— Marcus Aurelius

New Beginnings Every Day

Look, I know there are days, or weeks, or months when you feel like you've slipped off into a far off distant world. You can't find your way back and no one even seems to know you're there. You observe a community you're not entirely a part of, because these things they do and how they do them don't quite make sense to you, but still you find yourself stuck in these human habits and you rarely even notice them. Like how you wake up every morning and let an hour disappear in these well-shaped routines that you've spent years shaping, and you can do them in your sleep. No need to question it. A transportation from asleep to not quite so asleep. Or how you take the fastest way home even though it's 30 minutes of just trying to get home, because that's what you've always done. You watch the same TV-show, eat the same food from the same store because you've built a map of connections of how to get through the day without questions and it's all safe and calm. Still.

I once met a boy, at a bar, at 11 in the morning, when I was sad and heartbroken and thought that the bar at 11 in the morning was a safe place to be drunk and alone at, because normal people have places to go, things to attend, and I did not. But then there was this boy who walked in with a French beret and worn out Converse and ordered a 'bless the morning' drink together with a joke to the bartender, sat down beside me without hesitating, and started talking. Well, I was drunk and sad and wanted to be alone and this guy annoyed me and how rude to just sit down beside me without asking first and my bitter thoughts went on without hearing a word he said until I realised he'd gotten quiet, looking at me, waiting for my answer to a question I hadn't heard or honestly couldn't care less about. "Have you ever done that?" he repeated with a smile and his annoyingly colourful drink in his hand. I kept my eyes on my drink, hoping he'd get the hint, but this guy was not of my breed and before I knew it he'd grabbed my hand and off we went out on the streets. He walked fast and excited, still talking about this thing I obviously hadn't tried and that whiskey made my legs stumble as he nearly dragged me along.

Something happened, the seasons changed. Someone you thought you couldn't live without left. Or nothing happened. You slowly disappeared in the crowd on your way home every day. Too tired to be excited, or brave, or anything other than just tired. So that dream, that vision of who you wanted to be and where you wanted to go, slowly vanished along with your fire. No matter, you once had a crystal clear goal and a destination that made you wake up with eyes open wide every morning, and somehow you drifted further and further away from it, losing grip, sight, view. Life took you somewhere else, and now you curse your own luck and fate, because you have places you want to go and people keep telling you to be grateful and can't they see you're not where you're supposed to be, where you want to be?

I know. I've been there. But I'm here to tell you that you are exactly in the right place. At the right time. Doing the right thing. Being the right person. Even if you can't see that now.

Let me explain:

Today, August 17th 2014, is exactly 4 years since I stepped on that airplane from Sweden to London, ready to start over and build a life for myself that I wanted to wake up to every morning. I was young and naive and if I met that girl now I would try to save her from herself. I was lost, which is why I'm writing this. I was lost, but I had not yet learned to love uncertainty and mysteries, so I was scared and sad and had no idea how to survive another month because all I wanted to do was to write my music and live my words and find people who understood what it meant, to let me know that I was not alone. But where to even start?

Slowly and struggling I made my way through six months, which came to be the first six months of what I now consider my journey, my real life, "that's when it all changed" kind of thing. Going through my diaries I find at least 30 different 'final' goals and plans, the ones I thought would last forever, written by the girl I thought I'd always be. I was determined to not let anything make me change direction or avert my eyes, and I knew where I was headed.

But life is not a static object or one-way-street. It's a forever growing movement, a fleeting process that will flow in whichever direction it can, just because it simply can, and I'd like to mention trusting your fate. Every single time something crashed my plans, my dreams, I was forced to write a new plan, new goals, and take a different road. I cursed the moon and the stars and all the people walking on this earth who were in my way, because I thought I was being challenged. I thought I was being stopped from reaching my goal. But I can see it crystal clear now. Look back on your life, a month, six months, 10 years, and you will see how it all connects. Every time you were forced to change your ways it led you to something that led you to the next dot and suddenly you see how it's a beautiful well-crafted story with wonders and defeats, leaving and arriving, and that's why they call it a life story and not just a life. Life will keep redirecting you until you're on the right path, and it will feel like hurdles or obstacles in your way, but it's all in your favour. You just need to trust your story. Trust your path. Trust your place.

So I know you sometimes feel like you've lost track of that well-paved road you think you ought to take to get to where you want to be, but you're exactly in the right place exactly where you are. Trust the process of how things go and don't fight them, don't curse them. No story is worth telling without the twists and turns. Make them count instead.

Now go be where you are, and don't be sorry.

The boy in the bar, with me getting drunk at 11 in the morning, because I was heartbroken and sad, took my hand and dragged me along to the highest building in this town and showed me the hidden backdoor to the stairs that led us up to the roof, and the most magnificent view of this city. This city I came to call my home the next few months. We sat there the whole day, watching the world get busy and slow down, with the sun setting over the rooftops, and he barely knew my name and I didn't remember his, but it didn't matter. I said I liked sunsets and he said "you should see the sunrise," and told me about open fields in Canada, where he'd been. I listened and he talked and my broken heart ached a little lower and not so hard, and I never told him about it, but I think he knew, for by the end of the night he said he liked that I finally smiled and told me to do so more often, and that was just one of many days that didn't turn out the way I had planned, but just like I needed it to, and that's where I'd like to live.

So it's about the endless possibility of every single day.

Be always on your way.

"Dwell on the beauty of life.
Watch the stars, and see yourself running with them."
— Marcus Aurelius

The Simple Pleasure of Being Alive

I want to take long walks in the middle of the night without wondering what time it is, with nowhere to end up. Lie on empty streets and have a warm hand to hold when it gets cold, to walk home slowly. I want to go to Tuscany and sip red wine with the view of open fields and some old blues record played softly from a distance. I want to wake up early to the smell of freshly brewed coffee on a Sunday morning with someone beautiful to share it with. I want to take trains to new cities and spend afternoons in old book shops, those rare finds with one single owner who took over the shop after his great, great grandfather who once opened it and knew the name of every single author, book and customer. I want to learn about old writers and poets, how they lived and why they lived that way. And if they got a second chance, what would they change? I want to pack a suitcase with a few things I can't live without and give the rest to charity, then take a train to nowhere and everywhere and be happy wherever I end up. I want to ask the lonely man in the corner of the pub if I can join him for a whisky, and then spend the evening talking about what it means to love and lose and exist. Or just about the newest article in the local newspaper, or about roses and butterflies. Oceans and leavings. I want to write long handwritten letters to the ones I've left behind, telling them that I went away and probably won't be coming back, for a while, at least, because I never meant to stay in the first place and so you don't have to worry, I always find my way somehow. I want to spend a winter in a cabin in the forest, recording my next album. Near a lake somewhere in Scotland, with the crisp air in the morning and the fire every night as the only source of light to guide me through the discovery of new melodies and worlds, memories and stories.

It's so easy to wake up out of routine, make living a habit, and then find yourself drifting, daydreaming, not really here. But the world is endless and all you have to do is step outside and there it is, the endless possibilities of every single day.

I'll be chasing the horizon for the rest of my life.

Epilogue

The pages are turning, like they always do this time of year, and I wasn't really prepared
I think
for it scares me, the thought of being lifted from the roots again,
the roots I somehow unconsciously planted somewhere along the line
and now they all pull my hair, ripping my clothes and screaming GO GO GO!
So I open my eyes, still weary from too little sleep but still more than enough
and off I go.

Off I go.
It's time to keep moving.
It's always time to keep moving.

Don't be scared, I'm with you.

***

"Live! Live the wonderful life that is in you! Let nothing be lost
upon you. Be always searching for new sensations.
Be afraid of nothing."
— Oscar Wilde, *The Picture of Dorian Gray*

ABOUT THE AUTHOR

Charlotte Eriksson is a songwriter, producer, writer and publisher from Sweden, currently living somewhere in Europe, wherever the music plays at the moment. She left everything she had and knew as a teenager, and moved to London to dedicate her life to her music and art. Since then she has started her own publishing and distribution company *Broken Glass Records*, written three books (*Empty Roads & Broken Bottles; in search for The Great Perhaps, Another Vagabond Lost To Love*, and *You're Doing Just Fine*), and produced & released 5 EPs and 2 LPs under the artist name The Glass Child. She has previously been published on sites like Rebelle Society, Luna Luna Magazine and Germ Magazine etc.

AUTHOR NOTE

Dear you, I want to you know, talk to you, find you. Please say hi to me online, send me a picture of you and this book, or tell me about a memory you'll never forget. And if you liked my story, my journey, and want to help me tell the world about it, it would mean the whole world if you wanted to write a few nice words about this book as a review on Amazon & Goodreads.com, and tell all your friends, family, classmates and enemies about it. But most of all, go out and take your place in the world, for only you can fill it.

I'm nothing without you, but together we can help each other belong.

Thank you for being you.
Charlotte

Because I Love You ...
(and because by reading this book and my words, you've held my heart
in your hand) I have a little gift prepared for you.
If you go to: www.TheGlassChild.tumblr.com/FromMeToYou
you can get the first part of my other book
"Empty Roads & Broken Bottles; in search for The Great Perhaps",
for free straight to your email right away.
I hope you will like it

I also have another book called
"*You're Doing Just Fine*", that you might like.
You can read all about it on my website
www.CharlotteEriksson.com
There you will also find excerpts, quotes and some pictures of my books.

www.twitter.com/justaGlassChild
www.instagram.com/justaglasschild
www.facebook.com/TheGlassChild
www.TheGlassChild.tumblr.com
www.youtube.com/aGlassChild
TheGlassChildMusic@gmail.com

In my little store you can find personal framed art-prints with some of
my favorite quotes from this book. There you can also get signed copies
of any of my books, signed CDs, t-shirts and other fun things.
Go here to take a look: www.theGlassChild.bigcartel.com

Love always,
Charlotte

20891161R00074

Made in the USA
Middletown, DE
11 June 2015